John Charles Cooper
8-4-77

FINDING A SIMPLER LIFE

FINDING A SIMPLER LIFE

JOHN C. COOPER

A PILGRIM PRESS BOOK
FROM UNITED CHURCH PRESS
PHILADELPHIA

Copyright © 1974 by John C. Cooper
All rights Reserved

No part of this publication may be reproduced, stored in a retrieval system, or transmitted in any form or by any means, electronic, mechanical, photocopying, recording, or otherwise, without the prior permission of the publisher.

Library of Congress Cataloging in Publication Data

Cooper, John Charles.
  Finding a simpler life.

  "A Pilgrim Press book."
  Includes bibliographical references.
  1. Simplicity. 2. United States—Civilization—1945-   I. Title.
BJ1496.C66   917.3'03'92   74-7294
ISBN 0-8298-0281-9

United Church Press, 1505 Race Street,
Philadelphia, Pennsylvania 19102

For Bill Buchanan and Jim Bowers,
and in memory of Leo T. Hendrick,
examples of that combination of
intelligence and sensitivity we
pay honor to in this book

CONTENTS

Introduction   11

CHAPTER 1. The Pride of Possession   15

CHAPTER 2. The Revolt Against Conformity   27

CHAPTER 3. The Reaction Against
Both Conformity and Revolution   45

CHAPTER 4. Two Cultures in Collision   69

CHAPTER 5. Art and the New Plainness   87

CHAPTER 6. Feed Your Head—
A Natural Philosophy   105

Notes   125

INTRODUCTION

How Much Land Can a Man Use?

The famous Russian moralist and novelist, Count Leo Tolstoy, once put the view of the Plain Person very succinctly in a short story entitled "How Much Land Does a Man Need?" The tale involves a distribution of land to tenant farmers who are told that they may claim as much land for themselves as they can walk around in a day. One farmer paces himself and compasses a considerable piece of good land without overtiring himself or violating the time limit. Another man, however, lusts after as much land as he can possibly get. He drives himself to run all day over hill and valley, always seeing one more treasure—a well, a creek, a mountain—that he would like to own. Even as evening approaches, the man keeps pushing on, forgetting that he must run back to the starting point to have gone around his chosen plot. Finally, sweating and anxious in his selfishness, the farmer drops dead of overexertion. The writer echoes the haunting question, "Just how much land does a man need?"

Many North Americans are experiencing the twinge of that very same question today. Like the rich fool (Luke 12:16-21) many of us sit in comfortable, well-furnished houses with bulging savings and an echoing vacuum where meaning and happiness should be. Just how much land, how many rooms, how much savings, how many memberships, does anyone need?

The crushing suffocation of possessions and debts suddenly strikes a multitude of persons in middle life—taking them by the throat, choking off their breath in a kind of spiritual emphysema. How long, these people begin to wonder, do I have to lay by stores for tomorrow? When will that rainy day on which I will be free to enjoy the fruits of my labors ever come? Perhaps, it begins to dawn on them, perhaps we would have more of happiness if we had less of things. Perhaps the quantity of life and the quantity of things have little to do with the quality of life. Perhaps, but it is also possible and important for us only after we have been built up to a quantitative level that satisfies all of life's basic needs. The real answer to Tolstoy's question is: "A man needs just as much land (money, houses, etc.) as is necessary to support him in a fulfilling, responsible life. A man needs at least that much, although he really doesn't need more."

Moving Forward by Slowing Down

H. G. Wells, the famous novelist and critic of modern society, had a profound distrust of what the earlier part of our century called "progress." He regularly predicted the wars and social dislocations that have plagued our historical period. He looked with pessimistic eye on everything that developed in science, politics, and finance. He was convinced that no matter how innocent the invention or discovery, men would soon find a way to destroy each other with it.

Besides Oswald Spengler, Wells had few people to agree with him, although millions enjoyed reading his outrageous prose. Now, in the 1970's, millions of people everywhere have come to share Wells's and Spengler's pessimism about modern society. One such individual is a close friend of mine. Chuck is well established, well educated, and creative, yet he seems burdened with a wry pessimism about the national future as well as about the progress of his profession. He rather seriously expects a major economic depression (he is surely not alone in that) and is taking measures to prepare for it. This man reasons that land is the ultimate source of value. He has therefore acquired additional land near his home instead of making other investments. With the continual rise of inflation, Chuck has taken steps to move forward by slowing down the normal activities of his profession and class. Instead he has undertaken avocational farming, on a rather large scale for a city dweller, putting in many varieties of fruit trees besides a magnificent kitchen garden. Chuck has dug in to prepare for losses of employment, food scarcity, and financial disaster. Visiting him (and getting some of the produce for myself), I found Chuck pessimistically happy. Like the eternally bullish traders on the demoralized stock market, Chuck has discounted—in advance—everything but the end of the world. Standing by his corn, picking tomatoes, peppers, beans, peas, watermelons, muskmelons, potatoes, sweet potatoes, onions, and other foods, one can see the reality of living a plainer life without moving or drastically altering one's place in life. It is possible to adopt many of the features of the new-old pioneering life-style while remaining in town and at your usual job. Becoming a new pioneer is, first of all, a change in values and the acquiring of a new mentality—that is more important than moving to the woods.

Cutting Loose, Breaking Out Toward Freedom

Every social crisis is, in the final analysis, a crisis of the individual human spirit magnified millions of times. All the social experimentation that has gone on in the adoption of not one but a multitude of alternative life-styles since the middle 1960's has been the result of a psychic shock of recognition on the part of North Americans of all ages everywhere. What has actually transpired is the growth of awareness in millions that they are not doing what they want to do (but what others thought they should do) and that they are not living as they really want to live. Dorothy Kalins makes this exercise of freedom on the part of individuals very clear in her recent book, *Cutting Loose*,[1] and Harry Browne has spelled out this thirst for personal freedom in detail in *How I Found Freedom in an Unfree World*.[2] Browne blatantly (and necessarily) declares: "You are the ruler of your world and no one . . . can stop you from living as you want—unless you disregard your own sovereignty."[3]

Interestingly enough, those who are cutting loose to find their personal freedom are usually successful members of the system—not losers. Those who take the risk of doing the unpopular stunt of seeking less status and less wealth do so from a base of success in whatever position they formerly held in society. The new pioneers are seeking the plainer life for different reasons than the motives of the Amish (the original "plain people") who fled Europe to escape persecution and to live separately and righteously in an impure world. They are also differently motivated than the millions of poor Irishmen and Russian Jews (and others) who came to America to escape a losing situation in their homelands. The new wave of simplicity is composed of people moving from strength (in "establishment" terms) to strength (in terms of their own goals and desires). Therefore the attraction of the plainer life is psychological (even spiritual) not economic—or even political—in its primary foundations. That means we must constantly keep the difference between this return to the land movement and the drive to fill up the empty spaces of nineteenth-century America and Canada before our eyes as we assess this new life-style.

CHAPTER 1
THE PRIDE
OF POSSESSION

Until a very few years ago there was little doubt in anyone's mind that physical handsomeness or beauty was to be desired over physical plainness. Few people would have seen the slick form of the beautiful presented to us in magazine advertisements, in films, and on television programs as inherently less desirable than plainness in bodily makeup and dress. Many people still live within the context of the *Playboy* conception of the beautiful woman and the *Esquire* conception of the well-dressed man, but an increasingly large number of younger people are rejecting such standards of attractiveness as "plastic" and unreal. Hollywood still grinds out models of a too perfect beauty, pumping this ideal into every home through television, but millions of Americans have turned off the impact of such symbolism on them and are now in pursuit of a more wholesome, "natural," and readily available plainness.

Why such a change? The cosmetic industry has gone through one technological revolution after the other, providing both males and females with wigs, nail polishes, false moustaches and sideburns, as well as skin creams, hair dyes, and even surgical operations to overcome the effects of aging. At a time when young women do dress almost exactly like their male counterparts and when extremely informal costumes have become standard for day and night wear, we must recognize that the plastic-perfect good looks of the Hollywood actor and actress remains the ideal of millions. Proof of this lies in the news reports of governmental officials having their faces lifted and undergoing hair transplants.

Styles of beauty do change, however. We view photos of the bathing beauties of the 1890's with a good deal of humor today. It is hard for us to realize that a human epoch so close in time to our own put a premium on plumpness in women. Similarly, the "boy-girl" slimness of the "flapper" era in the 1920's with its "no-bosom" look also seems strange when we measure it either against the plastic paintedness of the 1940's or the no-bra look of today. We may still have a large following for the Hollywood look, but the <u>age of plainness has definitely set in</u>.

The style of beauty I call Hollywood plastic is best seen in Marilyn Monroe and in the contemporary actress, Raquel Welch. This vision of the beautiful is more than a fad; it is rather the dominating image of a dominant philosophy for thirty years, from the end of the Great Depression to the beginning of the Vietnam era. It was and is the popular symbol of the "get-rich-quick," "bigger is better," pansexuality of America's materialistic, civic religion. As such a heavy symbol, the Hollywood beauty image, even now when it is on the wane, has something to tell us about ourselves.

The Only Life Worth Living

Symbols are living structures. They are not invented, nor can they be manufactured. Pseudosymbols may be thrown out by advertising agencies, by movie directors, by popular preachers. But not one of the pseudosymbols will last for long or have great impact unless it somehow turns out not to have been superficial at all but to have struck some deep psychological chord in the minds of thousands of people. When this happens, and it has happened through films and even in commercial advertising, there is no question of falseness, but rather of recognizing a genuine symbol.

A symbol is the coalescence in finite form of an awareness of the process of man's psychic life, and specifically the statement of a recurring pattern of the reception of life's processes by the human consciousness. Such symbols arise in chance events, and upon reception by a larger social group, become hinges of history. They may grow out of the artistic creative process, including that of films and the popular writer of commercials, but only by chance, or in religious terms, by an act of grace. Symbols may also grow out of the residual spirituality and creativity of the general population. Undoubtedly a symbol must have the possibility of being widely communicated or else it will lack the possibility of becoming the property of a significant part of the human race.

The fact is that the dominant symbol of beauty in both its feminine and masculine aspects and the symbol of the life worth living, the ideal of courage, etc., do come into clear focus through the mass media of entertainment in each of the decades in our century. Specifically, the Hollywood image of beauty is an expression of a belief in philosophical hedonism and economic imperialism. It sees the good life as one that strives toward more and more sensual enjoyment and the seeking of ever greater amounts of wealth to support such pleasure. The vision of simplicity as innocence and of sin as sophistication is carried through in the critique of the city as the seat of evil by Jacques Ellul.[1] However, no criticism of urbanization or technology that simply assumes that development is the development of evil can ever be taken seriously by modern man. This is the case because modern man is dependent on technological sophistication for his survival. Primitive agriculture and handicraft industries cannot support 3½ billion plus people.

We still must look for a deeper meaning within the new vogue for plainness. If there is not a deeper conception than that of the Lost Paradise myth, then the quest for plainness is irresponsible, escapist, and even destructive.

Daniel Yankelovich, writing in *The Saturday Review*,[2] speaks of "the new naturalism." He places a high valuation on this "new naturalism" saying: "Our children are urging us to stop our frantic rush to bend nature to the human will and to try instead to restore a vital—and more humble—balance with nature."[3]

Among the marks of the new naturalism, Yankelovich sees an emphasis on the interdependence of everything in nature, the placing of sensory experience before intellectual knowledge, the desire to live close to the land, the wish to live in groups with other people, the thrust to reject hypocrisy, and the de-emphasis of science.

Such a protest is indeed now being made, and in the aesthetic realm it is directed against the American myth communicated to the masses by Hollywood. Hollywood, for many years, laid before the American public the ultimate symbol of the American dream. This symbol consisted of an almost perfect beauty of the starlet and the star, the handsomeness and courage of the great actors, and the quest, shown in their lives, to reach the top by whatever means; to become successful, to become wealthy. So much has been written about the beauty of the Hollywood starlet that we will not repeat it here. A good deal has been analyzed concerning Marilyn Monroe and the tragedy of her life, implying, rather directly, that her tragedy grew out of the manipulation of her natural beauty and the exploitation of her sex appeal for commercial gain. This is probably all quite true. However, here we do not so much want to analyze the plastic beauty, the unreal perfection of the Hollywood starlet. Rather, we would like to ask ourselves just what is there in this image that has attracted us for so long? What is involved in it that seems now to be rejected by many people in our society?

The beauty of Marilyn Monroe and Raquel Welch serve as good examples because they are examples of the lucky or fortunate person. They represent that one person, perhaps one out of a thousand, who was born perfectly formed, and whose beauty has been smoothed and enhanced by all sorts of sophisticated techniques. Whatever else they may be and symbolize, the beautiful stars and starlets of Hollywood's great period are anything but the girl next door. The beauty that they present is that of perfection or that approximating perfection. It represents both the perfection of evolved humanity and the perfection of a highly evolved technology. Taken in this light we can see developing through the star's image the idea that somehow the finest and noblest, the most spiritual, is that which has evolved and is highly sophisticated. This aesthetic symbol stands in contrast to the idea that somehow the sophisticated is evil and the plain or natural is spiritual or good.

However, the Hollywood screen presents an ambivalent attitude toward the too perfect beauty. It presents, for example, Ava Gardner, with her smooth good looks, as the ultimate symbol of sex and desirability. But, by the same token, it often presents such beauties as undergoing reversal, disaster, disease, and death. Hollywood often presents sophisticated beauty as somehow an act of hubris, an act of overweening pride against society or the Divine, or both. This is an interesting point. There is buried deep in the Hollywood catalog of films, from the very first even up to the movies of the 1970's, a kind of built-in morality. Many people might scoff at this code, but nevertheless, as crude and wooden as it is, it is there. Marilyn Monroe's life, both on camera and off, is a kind of myth, a kind of morality tale that symbolizes the ambivalent attitude of the Hollywood screen to the too perfect beauty, to the ultimate in handsomeness, to the ultimate in hubris, to the consummate in perfection. "Be careful lest you fly too near the sun" is the moral of many American films.

Economic Implications of the Near-perfect Beauty

We have mentioned that Hollywood does more than present to us the unattainable goal of personal beauty. Hollywood, more than anything else, including wartime propaganda or revolutionary fervor, has given us the philosophy of and an invitation to the American way of life. It has been the legitimate stage, not the film, that has raised an objection to the idea that those who strive and work hard, those who put up a good appearance and constantly play all the angles, will succeed. *Death of a Salesman* was a Broadway play before it was a Hollywood movie. On screen it is those who use their raw courage, in the case of the Western, or those who use their minds, in the case of urban-oriented movies, who make themselves a place in the sun of the American social scene.

The American dream, the presentation of oneself at the ultimate in possibility in a land where everything is open if one will take it, seems to be the gist of the Hollywood philosophy. Even those films which do not show this "getting ahead" kind of syndrome really reenforce us by showing us the unfortunate or unwarranted circumstances that present themselves to some men and women, forestalling their achievement of success. For example, all the gangster films from the 1930's and early 1940's show that, because of their ethnic background, because of their lack of education and their misguided direction in life, the main characters must fail and fall either to the policeman's bullet or to life in jail. Many times it is shown that they would have made a good life if they had used their driving energies in ways which were not forbidden by the law.

The Westerns, from the start and almost to the present, have been dramas of the American way of life. There, on the backdrop of wide open spaces of desert, sagebrush, and plains, against the backdrop of tall mountains, men and women dig out for themselves a new and richer style of life. But some fall by the wayside, excluded from success, more often than not, by their own character flaws. Those who lack faith, stamina, and drive fall by the trail, like the famous Donner party going through the Humboldt Sink toward California. The roadsides of the majority of our Western dramas show us the bleak bones of the weak. The survival of the fittest, of the courageous and the hard-working, is the presentation of life that underscores the philosophy of these movies.

Only in the past two decades have the undergirding assumptions of the Hollywood movie been challenged by movies themselves. The rise of a kind of unmeltable ethnic group, the recognition that some people simply could not be sucked into the American process, has created in movies, as in life, a kind of alternative American life-style. We are now treated to ideas of beauty that are other than those given us in the flicks of the 1940's. We are now living in a time when the assertion that "black is beautiful" is a theme in many films. *Shaft* and *Shaft's Big Score* and more recent films are examples of this theme.

It is undoubtedly because of a change in the American social situation since World War II that not only have some of the movies themselves changed but our attitudes toward the symbols presented to us have changed too. It is interesting to note just what kind of movies are popular among young people in the 1970's. On the one hand there are the many kinds of countercultural films that try to reflect the drug subculture, long hair and the so-called natural way of life. Except for a few, these are very largely commercial exploitations of styles and fads rather than being deep statements of the countercultural emphasis. On the other hand, many young people seem tremendously drawn to some of the older films of the 1930's and 1940's. But they are not the films in which beautiful stars are portrayed. It isn't Rita Hayworth, or even Greta Garbo but Humphrey Bogart, Edward G. Robinson, and W. C. Fields, people that are not perfect beauties at all, who are popular. They are very common, ordinary looking kinds of people that are usually defeated. Again and again, people single out old movie anti-heroes and anti-heroines as their idols because they tend to be rebels, revolutionary types; people with whom they can identify. Humphrey Bogart is our hero and W. C. Fields, with his cynical rejection of middle-class morality, is our philosopher. We look for actors who are close to the common life of common people, and we identify with those who failed to reach the American dream.

The Turn Right

There is little doubt that the film in America has been used in a counterrevolutionary or reactionary social way. Films do have politics. The camera may be neutral, so that we may have a Russian director making a film glorifying socialism, or John Wayne making a film that glorifies the superiority of the American white male over all enemies: females, males, Blacks, Whites, foreign and domestic, but films do have politics. Today, revolutions are not popular, yet there is a silent turning off of the older themes of expansion, superiority, and getting rich quick that characterized the movies in America until recently. The symbols of beauty and handsomeness, the aesthetic of the American way of life, have been turned off today as well. However, there is still a large, wide reservoir of people who are not revolutionary or reactionary in their outlook, and for them Hollywood has turned out films which are still quite profitable. Films by John Wayne symbolize this. But, for the most part, the older films that lack the American superioristic vision are more popular among the young. Perhaps too much has been made of the drift toward conservatism in American institutions, but I personally do not think so. This drift, which has become a rush toward the right under the Nixon Administration, is remarkable considering the thrust leftward of the more liberal life-styles that have been the rule since World War II. In this regard, we will see in later chapters that the very aesthetic symbols of what is beautiful and what is right, in other words, both ethics and aesthetics, are protests against the kind of thinking that tries to turn the clock back in order to avoid the disconcerting events that have come upon us.

The pride of possession, the too perfect beauty of Hollywood in the 1930's, remains the typical symbol of the American expression of superiority. Interestingly enough, those persons symbolized as gods and goddesses of beauty and handsomeness were all white and always neat. Not even the turning away from the white powdered faces of the silent movies, toward the more natural makeup of the

1930's and 1940's has made much difference to the perfection of faces and body projected to us as examples to emulate and worship. They were all faces that were interchangeable in any decent company of American citizens. Even men, who show their courage and braveness by their tragic faces, have faces that are Anglo-Saxon, faces that represent the most traditional, conscious self-centeredness of the Northern European people.

In late years there has been some turning away from this, toward natural, everyday characters on the stage and screen. Not only has this turning been symbolized by the growing importance of black people in movies and stage plays, but also in the presentation to us, for example, of people who are less than perfect. You can check this trend toward naturalism by simply looking at the newer films shown during prime time on television, then watching the older movies on the late night television. There is at once a striking dissimilarity. The heroines of the older movies are different, not only because their skirts are longer or their hair is differently fashioned but because their whole appearance is different from the heroine of a recently made film. This is also true of our heroes. Even in the gangster movies and the spy films which make up so much of television fare, the quite ordinary hero rules today, too. Michael Caine is a good symbol of our period. Who would have ever thought of a James Bond-type secret agent wearing glasses? Yet Michael Caine is presented to us as a person who is lazy, not overly loyal, independent, and while serving the Establishment, nevertheless tends to be on the wrong side of his superiors. I see a kind of cynicism in this series, for he does serve the Establishment quite well, often sacrificing himself to save them, while at the same time, he pokes fun at his superiors. There is almost a draining away of the truth, of the resentment we have of being used by the Establishment through the actions of someone like Michael Caine. James Bond, on the other hand, is a throwback to older heroes of the film, someone almost transcendental in his handsomeness, and well-nigh supernatural in his cunning, his sexual powers, and his physical strength. But Bond is hard to take seriously.

He is as fake as the gadgets that are attached to his car and are given to him to track down his enemies. Michael Caine, for all the grandiosity of the plots in which he is involved, tends to be a human being, equipped sometimes with little radios but more apt to depend on a knife or a gun and his own feet to carry him through hard times.

The Too-perfect Beauty and Technology

This concoction of the ultimate in the feminine mystique, and for the male, the ultimate in handsomeness, is not just a production of nature but also of technology. The cosmetic industry must have gone through many changes and through many forms of development. We know about thousands of dollars spent in the capping and fixing of the teeth of movie actors. We know about the ingenious hair pieces, toupees, and wigs which are a part of their lives, just as they are a part of the life of many people in America in the middle-class. We know about the false lenses over the eyes to change their color. We know about operations to improve the quality of the skin by face lifting. The Watergate hearings have even let us know of devices that can change one's speech. We know that these and other kinds of techniques are used to produce this too-perfect beauty that has impressed us for so long, and which is still with us. Only among the young and some of their older allies has this imagery and symbolism been called in question. Among the middle class, or people who have moved into the middle class since World War II, the image of having just come from the beauty parlor is still a desirable one. Indeed, among the very poor there is no valuation of their rough clothing as stylish or mod. The way of smooth good looks and classy clothes appeals to the poor and is held on to by families that have only recently made the transition from poverty to the middle class. In fact, the most ragged clothing and scruffy appearances are seen on college campuses peopled by the children of the well-to-do, such as Antioch, Chicago, or Harvard. The absolutely lowest level of countercultural alienation in clothing style that I have observed was during a 1971 visit to Goddard College in Vermont.

The philosophy at Goddard can only be described as utterly "far out." Clothing styles ran to the most ragged jeans and hair styles to the longest and freakiest I have seen. Perhaps the nadir of countercultural styles was the group of students we saw working naked in their organic garden. Bent over, scratching at the ground with sticks, dropping seeds in the earth, these college students reminded me of the color photos of the savages in New Guinea that adorn the pages of *National Geographic*. I think I would be less harsh in my assessment if such a life-style contributed to the young people's creativity, study, and happiness, but conversations with faculty and students failed to give evidence of this, and even implied the converse.

Just what is involved in the rejection of the pride of possession, the too perfect beauty of Hollywood? Is it the rejection of the kind of imperialism implied in such standards of beauty? Is it the rejection of the overwhelming claims of American society and economics on our allegiance? Is it the rejection of the right of society at large to manipulate us into forms and shapes which we personally may not desire? Is it an assertion of individual freedom and liberty? I think it is all these things. For those who have been massaged by the educational process year after year, softened up and crunched and poked and shaped by television and radio, have now rebelled. The new emphasis on the natural is the way in which they can say *no* to outside pressures and *yes* to symbols that they have embraced freely for themselves. I think that neither those who share in the new mentality, on the left of society, nor those on the right of society who deplore the new images and long for the old, really understand that the simplest little things that we take for granted in the youth subculture are really laden, heavily freighted, with revolutionary or at least rebellious content. It is difficult to see this until you stand back and measure the new life-styles alongside the older generation, or until you contrast the movies in prime time against the older movies after midnight on television. Meanwhile, it remains true that the moustache and the beard and long hair—even excessively long hair on girls—is looked upon as a sort of rebellious symbol by multitudes in this country. It remains true that somehow the wearing of old clothes is looked upon as a rejection of the economic attainment of one's parents and of the culture at large. I have heard these words expressed by more than one parent on more than one occasion. "We work," they say, "we strive to make it possible for these children to have so much, to go to college, and make a good appearance, now look at the way they behave." Such an expression sounds fraudulent to many of us, but it is quite sincerely said. And it may be sincerely said by parents to children who have no such rebellious thoughts consciously in mind. They may simply be following their peer-group standards. But that is precisely the point, their peer-group's standards are standards of beauty and excellence, of handsomeness and of outlook that are rejective of the standards of the older generation.

In the chapters to come, we want to investigate the "skuzzy" style of life—a style which has now passed its peak and has tapered off and mellowed down in what I would call an age that has moved beyond beauty and luxury. In this age of plainness, naturalness and simplicity are prized and are expressed rather than a more overtly rebellious or rejective standard of behavior, dress, and conduct. Nevertheless, even the natural style—a style that is exemplified in the 1970's by the return of some styling of the hair, some haircutting among the men, as well as the continuing of long hair by others, remains as much a rejection of the pride of the past and the reactionary tendency in American society today as was the skuzziness of what some people called "those dirty hippies."

CHAPTER 2
THE REVOLT AGAINST CONFORMITY

Clothes, an old proverb tells us, do not make the man, but in late-twentieth-century America, clothes certainly seem to make a man what he is. All over the United States, parents, teachers, administrators and policemen have condemned the youthful style of dress that came to prominence in the early 1960's. This dress style, marked by worn and patched, faded blue jeans, old Army field jackets, grubby tee shirts, sandals (or bare feet), and assorted beads, has been called "hippy," "cruddy," "skuzzy," "grubby," "dirty," "in," and "beautiful." For the young it remains a kind of base standard against which to measure their own less drastic nonconformity. Blue jeans (a very expensive article of clothing for many young people) have an almost universal appeal and acceptability among young people, as do beads, tee shirts, knit shirts, vests, and jackets of better or worse material. Such articles make up the common dress of almost all the young. Pants may be of cotton or blue denim, or even double knit, but they must be flared, tapered, or decorated.

A long time ago, I began making notes about the changing dress styles of college young people. I believe I watched the changeover from relatively "straight" modes of dress to what I came to call "skuzzy," rather carefully. This change came in response to the splintering of traditional values that arose when the shortcomings of American society became apparent to all—during the time of the civil rights struggle. Suddenly young people of the middle class began to identify with the poor. The beat-up dress and careless grooming that became "in" had to do with a positive value placed on poverty and the simple life.

Give Me the Simple Life

It is amazing to experience how little is actually necessary to sustain an interesting and happy life. For the American of the middle class most of the challenge and color has been leached out of life. The routine of a daily job, the comfort of suburban living, the protection of the police—all these keep most of us from knowing what the majority of people in the world know—all we need is a place to sleep, a few clothes, something to eat, and some work or hobby to keep the mind and spirit alive.

The advent of the hitchhiking culture, the spread of reduced student air fares, and the sending of millions of young men to the Asian backwaters of the world has made millions of Americans aware of the possibility of a simpler, more satisfying life. The rise of concern over what technology is doing to the environment and the reaction of thousands of students against the artificiality of university life has made the search for the simple life more appealing.

I recall the "cities" built by refugees in Korea. Here life went on with a minimum of what we consider the necessities of life. The "hooches" or houses were built of scraps of lumber and tin. I remember one permanent structure that was covered completely with flattened beer cans—a metal building built completely out of the refuse of an army.

America, too, knows communities like that. One of them is John's Island, South Carolina, a locale just south of Charleston, along the Sea Island Coast. This is a nest of rural, black poverty, horrible enough in itself, and only a symbol of hundreds of other forgotten spots in the United

States. Located far off the main roads, reached by winding asphalt and dirt roads, John's Island is made up of one dilapidated shack after the other. There is no industry and no business beyond the "mom and pop" groceries found everywhere. The people live under physical conditions that would kill them if they were not in such a warm climate. In all events, their lives are full of hunger and of diseases already conquered in wealthier places.[1]

Skuzziness

Let me describe what I have labeled as a "skuzzy style of dress." Bear in mind that I am not being critical, for there is nothing in this style of dress that offends me personally. Indeed, most of my younger friends over the last decade have dressed in this way, and I have become so used to it that in many respects I have adopted parts of it for myself.

A skuzzy or hippie dress style is easily recognizable. The standard pants for men and women are blue jeans—the more faded and patched, the better. Oftentimes these blue jeans are sewn over with patches bearing various emblems and descriptions or are embroidered. Many times we see butterflies or peace symbols, or the famous figure of the marijuana smoker embroidered or stenciled on the trousers. They may be held up by hand-knitted belts or by wide leather belts; at times, even by ropes. On some young people there are leather thongs tied in the belt loops with little dangling bells or other ornamentation. Indeed, one of the farthest-out people I have ever known was a poet that I met "hitch-hiking" through the high Cascade Mountains in Washington, in 1968. He was marked, even in the distance, by jangling little Oriental bells hanging from the side of his trousers. Another thing often tied to the belt loops or else worn on the belt or from a shoulder strap is the little purse, sometimes called the stash bag because it is frequently used to stash marijuana, papers, or hash pipes. The shirt might be anything from an old tee shirt to a polo shirt, a gray workshirt, an old colored shirt, to an old Army shirt; oftentimes a checkered shirt. The older the shirt the better, for it will be decorated in time. Sometimes a collar is cut off, so that it has a clerical appearance. For a coat we often find old Army field jackets or even old Army great coats—the long heavy coats that are so serviceable. Young girls seem particularly intrigued with the long coats that reach to their feet. These are available at Army surplus stores or Salvation Army stores. Hats can be anything from nothing at all to old fedoras, to fezes or berets or Army barracks hats. I dare say that, on balance, most of the skuzzily dressed people I have known through this country and Canada have not worn hats at all, or else they wore wide-brimmed floppy hats, with or without feathers and other decorations. One's hair style will determine what kind of hat he wears. Long hair can easily be worn with the wide-brimmed floppy hat, but if one has an Afro or teased hair, any kind of hat is difficult to wear.

Let me describe one of my friends at a small Michigan college. He is a young man in his early twenties, quite attractive in a lot of ways, very intelligent and pleasant to know. His hair stands out from his head a foot and a half to two feet in length. It stands straight out and is very kinky, curly, and quite blond. His is an unusual head of hair, although it is perfectly natural. He simply let it grow and then teased it out with a comb. Being perfectly round, his hairdo makes him look like a saint surrounded by a halo. For shoes on a person like this or one who likes to be hip, you might find sandals, but the weather would determine that. Many times boots or old Army shoes are worn. Indian mocassins are quite popular among young girls but I haven't seen many boys wearing them. I would say that, of late, boots, riding types that zip up, lumberjack or parachute jump boots are more common than anything else. "Waffle stompers" or hiking shoes are popular throughout the West and around the Great Lakes. Hippie people dress in their own way all the time. They are ready, in all kinds of weather, to do any conceivable thing, consequently they are prepared with rough and ready clothes for whatever comes along.

Nostalgie de la boue

The movie *Butch Cassidy and the Sundance Kid*, which appeared a few years ago, represents a protest against the long-time Hollywood image of beauty, courage, and the American way of life. It is a revisionist Western movie, to be sure, but it also contains a strong sense of the alienation and lostness of the individual in a developed society. Butch and the Kid can no longer live in a West fenced in and crisscrossed with telegraph poles and railroad tracks. They rebel, violently, then they run away. Nothing really suffices, however, and they die.

In a real way this movie is founded on the "Lost Paradise" vision of what is good. The older, nondeveloped West is seen as a "better" world than the West of the railroad and advancing civilization. Butch and the Kid go to South America precisely to try to find an environment that will still be "wild" like the Old West. But "civilization" has reached Bolivia too.

In a far more direct way, *Butch Cassidy and the Sundance Kid* is a protest against the confining lineaments of present-day society. The young male heroes are mirror images, in hair, dress, speech, and moral outlook, of young college-age males today. The "skuzzy" look and the free speech of slang and four-letter words represent a protest against the oppressive weight of an overdeveloped society, just as they also constitute a kind of *nostalgie de la boue*. This means "nostalgia of the mud," or a sentimental valuation of past states of primitivism or poverty. One looks back, from this emotional perspective, on more free, more open societies, where there was room to roam, to be oneself and to make mistakes that were not recorded by interlocking authorities. Before, in the Old West, Butch and the Kid, very real outlaws, could break laws in one place and flee to another where they could take up the thread of their lives. They found that the telegraph had changed all that. Today, police computers work more thoroughly and thus limit the freedom of the second chance more completely.

The rise of the widespread usage of four-letter words (the

"filthy speech movement"), of social violence, and of drug usage are all somewhat related to *nostalgie de la boue*—even if this nostalgia is for a pseudopast as presented to us in films, novels, and on television. Our social behavior today seems to be patterned on past behaviors that arose in crisis situations, for example, during wars or during the settlement of frontiers. The popularity of "Army slang" (even among war resisters) and of old GI clothing seems related to this nostalgia for the supremely critical epoch (and thus the time when all traditional culture-guides were down) of the twentieth century—World War II. It may be strange to contemplate, but the heavy amount of exposure to material about World War II by people of the past several youth generations may have given them a nostalgia for what they (as nonparticipants) can only see as a terribly free period of history. Even those of us who are veterans can sense some of this, for, within the awful restrictions and limitations of war, there does arise an openness and freedom from irritating restraint (especially among combat troops or any overseas troops) that is experienced as exhilarating. Freud would understand the psychic joy that comes when the discontents of civilization are suspended for a time. The old saying that once you have committed murder, it is easy to break all the rest of the commandments is close to the mark.

That violence, especially guerrilla forms of violence, should arise out of such a nostalgia is easily proven. The glorification of the underground (urban) resistor against Nazism in every entertainment medium, as well as in existentialist philosophy, sets the stage for the secret soldier, the sniper and saboteur as the heroic symbol of our time. No wonder we have such an admiration, no matter how grudging, for the Viet Cong.

A moment's reflection demonstrates that violence, in its many forms, is a constant fact of American life. We have come to appreciate "institutionalized violence"—or the systematic exclusion of some people from rights and opportunities in our society. We need now to face up to "chucking it," "breaking free" and "cutting loose" as forms of violence (no matter how justified) also. To pick up and leave the

Establishment in order to find personal fulfillment in a new life-style is peaceful, to be sure, but it is a rejection of the status quo in America—and can be fully understood only when that is held in mind. The rejection of war as a possible social policy by millions of people is one of the most significant aspects of the Vietnam era. Nevertheless the popularity of war themes in books, movies, and on television shows that there is a residual fascination with killing and adventure even among a post-Vietnam population. As long as children play with toy guns and we ascribe respect to those who were "heroic" in war—or on police forces—we will probably retain this nostalgia for mass violence.

Violence and Haggling

I have commented upon violence at some length in my book *The Turn Right*[2] and Rollo May has given us an in-depth study of the sources of violence in *Power and Innocence*,[3] but we must mention some points here. There seems to be a connection, psychosocially, between random acts of violence, the rise of private bargaining (the garage sale), and the reaction that expresses itself in informal, very personal styles of dress. All these phenomena may be reactions against the sterile, nonhuman world of institutions, regulations, mass transport, and mass media we have built up in America. Men and women, young and old, may be digging out ways of attempting to become significant somebodies by increasing the human contact (and human notice) in their lives.

What is at issue here, in the significant social events of our lives, is the fact that a search for the simple life, for a status as plain persons, is a search for our lost sense of our own humanity. We seek to *announce* ourselves as real persons by dressing differently from the expected pattern. We seek to be taken seriously as persons—not just planned for consumers—in our private garage sale dealing. And for the greatly disturbed, we seek for human acknowledgment of our inner upset, unfortunately, in acts of violence and/or drug intoxication. Along the healthier route of skuzzy clothes and private bargaining, we seek to drop out of a computerized, indifferent culture in order to drop into the human race.

Methods of Protest That Say "I Am"

The last decade has seen the development of multiple forms of social protest, some silent, some very noisy, some peaceful, some not.

There has been the continuing protest against racism, which has won a verbal victory, in that the drive toward brotherhood has become integrated into the national rhetoric —without becoming fully actual, to be sure. There has been a nine-year protest against United States involvement in the Vietnam War—a protest that was not completely silenced even after the formal peace treaty signing of January, 1973. There has also been a very articulate attack on American social conformity that continues unabated. But it is only the intelligentsia that can make such a protest in abstract, literary ways. Most of us have protested conformity simply by refusing to conform and adopting alternative styles of life.

A news photo circulated in February 1973 showed a man in Pennsylvania who began protesting the Vietnam involvement in 1961 by letting his hair and beard grow. Here was a silent but visually effective nonconformity, for his hair was four feet long. Something like the same sentiment inspired the earliest "hippies" to grow beards and long hair, and a similar nonconformity inspired less agitated young people to emulate them during the past ten years.

Studies of the so-called generation gap and of the conflict between police and students have shown the inability of many older people to tolerate "rough" language from young people. Amazingly, policemen, whose own speech is often locker-room level, become enraged when young people hurl four-letter words at them. No doubt this thin-skinned reaction has fueled the filthy speech movement on some campuses and the nationwide deterioration of language among young people. It is fair to say that among the young and the liberal older people, four-letter words function as a normal part of speech, having lost their connotations. Such a process has always been the rule in armies and navies, on sports teams, and in factory work. Three years in the Marines taught me that so-called "cursing" simply becomes a social indicator, a mark that one belongs to an in-group. Parents and educators would do well to acknowledge this fact today. Even some younger clergymen, who share the new consciousness, speak in the same fashion.

Along the same line, the rise of hard rock, "rock-a-billy," folk rock, jazz rock and especially acid rock, has come as a protest against the homogenized American culture that the young reject. That rock music is the cultural matrix of the young is not a debatable assertion. Young people expend more effort, energy, time, and money on rock music than on any other activity.

It is not surprising that so many of the rock stars are identified with various protest movements. Nor is it odd that youth music festivals have raised so many hackles on the necks of older people. One Woodstock does not a nationwide acceptance make. In 1972, for example, the good citizens of a northwestern Ohio town finally succeeded in warping rules and regulations to drive a youth music festival out of business. "The Park," like hundreds of other enterprises all over the country, gave the young a place to hear, play, and enjoy their culture. It was declared a menace to health and morals and closed. "The Park" was at least a menace to conformity.

Negative Nonconformity

Besides social violence, which has been done to the younger bearers of a new mentality more than they have ever done it to others, there are two other negative nonconformistic movements or activities in present-day culture. Both have relatively understandable origins, both can be vastly overrated in terms of social harm, but both can quickly become truly destructive for those who embrace them. The first is the misuse of drugs. The second is the rise of occultism.

Drugs and the Search for the Natural

The American way of life, in general, did not contain much belief in the efficacy of drugs, despite their occurrence in earlier American history. Drugs played a role in the nineteenth century, coming into use during the Civil War when they were given rather indiscriminately to wounded persons in such a way that many became addicts. This form of medical addiction was never widely recognized and indeed the failure to recognize this danger led to the indiscriminate use of opiates in patent medicines throughout the last part of the nineteenth and early part of the twentieth centuries.

No one, before the rise of the counterculture, would have considered taking drugs as a return to nature or part of the natural way of life, despite the fact that herbs played a role in the simpler rural life of the frontier. Indeed, most utopians who were looking for a more natural way of life rejected even alcohol, thinking that the natural was very much involved in keeping clear of foreign substances. The Amish rejection of tobacco and alcohol is part of this pattern of "temperance." That this form of positive valuation of the natural was strong in older America is demonstrated by the support given Prohibition.

The identification of the counterculture with a positive attitude toward drugs comes, then, as a shock to all the traditional values in America. Aside from the fact that people may find sensual pleasure, at least for a time, in drug-taking, one can only see this embracing of dope as an expression of extreme rejection of the culture around us. It amounts to an identification not only with the proletariat but with the criminal underground of the large cities. It is a very definite *no* to the traditional ideas of beauty, good, health and sobriety. It implies an altogether different form of consciousness. One of the posters at the Harvard student strike during the turbulent 1960's said, "We must protect our drug culture." This expression shows the almost complete identification of the new counterculture (in some minds) with the drug subculture, an identification that is legitimately made only in some areas. I hope to show in this book that such a complete identification is wrong.

The revolt against conformity expressed in the drug subculture has both a negative and a positive pole. The negative pole, of course, can be seen as the ultimate rejection of the ordinary form of consciousness, expressed in a desire to remain as intoxicated as possible for as long as possible. That this is a deadend which can lead to no new form of culture would seem to need little documentation. How can one create anything if he is unable to navigate, much less think? We have reports of young people and older people who felt they were going to break through to the core of creativity in themselves by way of drug use. They would attempt to write while in a "stoned" condition. After all, Edgar Allan Poe had done as much, and Samuel Taylor Coleridge had had streaks of genius under drugs. Such people forgot that Coleridge never finished "Kubla Khan." Indeed, few of our modern drug creators have finished anything. One young man reported that he would think that he was writing reams and reams of paper on his novel and would later find he had only scrawled on a pad. Such creators forgot that even Hemingway, who had the writer's typical disease, alcoholism, would write early in the morning and would only start drinking in the afternoon after his work for the day was done.

On the positive pole, drug-users in the counterculture have been able to point to the assistance of drug experiences in helping them break through their cultural hangups and see their life situations more clearly. The chief figure of this drug outlook is the famous anthropologist Carlos Castaneda. Castaneda has given us three important and exciting books about the world of sorcery and Indian medicine in his studies of Don Juan: *The Teachings of Don Juan, A Separate Reality,* and *Journey to Ixtlan.*[4]

I speak of the interest in drugs and the counterculture that is connected with the desire for the recovery of a more human form of existence as a positive pole, although I realize that in the hands of the young it is a dubious proposition. The underlying drive of the plain person, for the recovery of the natural, is widespread in present-day culture.

Millions are searching for a regenerative principle in their daily lives. Considering the backdrop of the overwhelming American belief in the efficacy of medicine it is not surprising that this search would take the form of an excursion into drugs. As has been pointed out by many commentators, American society has become one in which there is a widespread belief that there is a chemical additive that will cure any problem. Among all levels of our society there is the use of alcohol for "attitude adjustment" and for relaxation after work. Physicians have gone a long way toward creating a general drug culture by a heavy-handed use of prescriptions for tranquilizers for many family and psychological problems. Mass advertising has offered the public more and more complex formulas to improve people's disposition, their looks, and their situation in the world. Why should we be surprised when young people decide about marijuana that "God grows his own" and that it is much more natural and healthy than many of the "straight" preparations?

Additionally, there is a literary tradition of experimenting with drugs that is much more cogent than the case of Coleridge. Aldous Huxley experimented with a number of substances in his efforts to open the doors of perception. The idea that somehow we could get back to our essential selves by turning on was well established long before the rise of interest in the writings of Castaneda.

The Occult

I have discussed the rise of occultism in *Religion in the Age of Aquarius*,[5] so I will not go into the topic here at length. However, occultism is one of the paths by which a large number of people today are seeking both to revolt against the conformity of our mass culture and to discover some connection with the natural, human world.

One may find it difficult to see the positive thrust in the attraction of the occult as well as in uncovering the final negative or demonic danger that lies in it. Obviously, searching in the occult shows a rejection of the standard religious culture. One does not seek only to be radical in his approach to religion, but even to go outside the bounds of what has been the mainline of Western faith for eighteen hundred years. However, on the positive side it must be pointed out that occultism was a rural phenomenon for centuries and it retains (almost alone in the area of religion) an interest in plants, herbs, and man's supposed connection with nature. For the person who is into the occult there is a stress upon the universal interconnection of all living beings that they have not experienced in their mainline religion. Christianity has this stress and depth but it has not been part of the normal message of either Catholicism or Protestantism for several centuries. Additionally, entrance into occultic practices immediately makes one a part of an in-group that is usually tight-knit and separated by bonds of secrecy from the mass culture around us. Taking on the trappings of a witch or warlock, and certainly of a Satan worshiper, makes one a member of the counterculture in no uncertain terms.

But there is a very dangerous and negative possibility at the heart of occultism. This judgment is not made theologically but psychologically and socially. Occultism taken too seriously—and we recognize that most people do not take it seriously—leads into a fantastic world that bears little relationship to the world that we must deal with every day. It gives its guidance on the basis of a traditional set of answers that is based on sympathetic magic, which is an utterly false view of the universe. The serious occultist becomes separated from the world and falls into a general schizophrenia. Ultimately the theological and ethical drawbacks must become clear to all. Persons divorced from reality are neither able to help themselves nor their neighbors. The state of the person lost in occultic reverie is not utterly different from the fundamentalist who also gets lost in a biblical reverie which is equally out of touch with reality. Psychologically, the illness involved in this is clear—one is schizophrenic or separated from reality, not responsive to real problems; theologically, the illness is idolatry—one worships a false god or gods basically because one lives in a false world. In both cases, the spirit is as dead as in any drug addict or suicide.

A Positive Evaluation

It should be clear that there are some difficult aspects to the revolt against conformity as well as some heartening ones. A true appreciation of the counterculture which has developed in our time will be balanced with an analysis of the defective features in it as well as giving an appreciation of the positive side of it. If we are to truly improve the quality of human life then such honesty is necessary. The truth, in the sense of a picture of how things really are, never asks through whose mouth it is being voiced. To point out the negativities in the counterculture, as is done by some conservatives, without pointing out the human advances in it is to imply that all is for the best in our society in the best of all possible worlds. Such a belief is nonsense. A protest was needed and it is needed still in America and throughout Western civilization. The image of the beautiful as presented by Hollywood is simply washed away in the revolution against conformity. The heroes of this countercultural style are those who are unprepossessing in physical beauty, grace, and language. There is an overemphasis on the ugly. The hippie life-style is one that directly pokes fun at the middle-class preoccupation with cleanliness. Ugly situations are evoked, as with confrontations with the police, demands for reforms of the penal system, the bringing of homosexuality into the open, the glorification of drug use, openness concerning sex, the use of words thought to be forbidden, and a general flaunting of the so-called social amenities. Undoubtedly there was an overreaction in some of this. Young people and their older sympathizers began to think of themselves as freaks. This word is well chosen, and it undoubtedly grew out of the counterculture itself to denote both their well-nigh absolute difference from straight society as well as pointing up the small number of freaks (like people in a side show) over against the vast population looking on. Beneath all this carnival spectacle, which is slowly passing into history now, lay far deeper social implications than are generally realized. It is these implications that, having now been stated, form the positive contribution the revolution in life-style has bequeathed to us. We will only mention them here and develop them in the next chapter.

The major implications of the revolution is first the declaration that there is a crisis of authority in Western culture. The force of moral persuasion that operates in a healthy culture has drained away. No longer was a system of relations among people functioning. The sign of this has been the eruption of violence and a call for law and order. We must see that the overuse of force to control social situations is not a mark of a functioning authority, but of an absence of authority. A family in which children are beaten continually, or held in line by threats of force, is one where parental authority has disappeared. A state in which the police must enforce the laws with frequent use of weapons is one where the citizens no longer recognize the authority of the government. No portion of the globe has been more heavily policed than Europe under Hitler, yet no reasonable person would claim that a healthy authority situation existed there. The freaks and the hippie revolution graphicly pointed out that the emperor had no clothes; that the major institutions of our society had lost much of their authoritative appeal to the young and sensitive.

The second implication of the revolution in life-style was that the image of too perfect beauty from Hollywood, stressed in mass advertising, held up as a standard for middle-class taste, was inhuman and destructive of human happiness. Not only the giving up of dresses and cosmetics for dirty blue jeans, bralessness, and unshaven legs by young girls pointed this out. The life experience of Marilyn Monroe is a graphic symbol of the ultimate dehumanization that lies at the base of the idea that smooth features and good grooming are the secret of happiness. The later counter-cultural development of women's liberation with its stress on the misuse of a female as a sex object is a valid lifting up of this truth. However, what Women's Liberation sometimes misses is the dehumanization and exploitation of the male, as well as the female, by this dominant archetype. The male is trapped into the tight society, chained to the circular treadmill of the acquisitive society by the idea that only by achieving financial and social success, that is, by conforming, can he have an example of such perfect beauty for his very own. Without intending a pun, the ultimate prostitution of what society does with the Hollywood idea of beauty is seen in the five-hundred-dollar-a-night price tag placed on the most attractive prostitutes. This seems to say that the ultimate possession of the outstanding American symbol is only through money and thus only open to the successful businessman. Imagine the shattering impact of the counterculture theme of free love on this situation. Therefore, the social revolution's emphasis upon openness to each other, even in sexual matters, is an overwhelming economic, as well as social and moral, critique of the American way of life.

The third implication of the revolution in life-styles is that the widely spread movement toward human liberation that rose up in the midst of World War II and spread to former colonies in Asia and Africa afterward, is a movement that is needed in North America, too. The freaks and hippies, even in their more unpolitical attributes, represent by their identification with the nonmiddle class a form of the Third World in the midst of Western society. One thing that was clear from the beginning in the movement I first called the "new mentality" and others have called the "counterculture" was that it was a revolution of decreasing expectations and a form of social progress by subtraction. In this way, the later developed interest in ecology was tied to a key feeling in the hippie life-style. It is difficult for most people to see the decreasing expectations among the freaks because we seem to naturally fasten upon the different cultural artifacts they displayed. People noticed the flowers, beads, peace symbols, water pipes, painted Volkswagen buses, and other exterior ornaments of youth culture. What was not noticed was all the things that were missing—the good furniture, the electrical appliances, the fine clothes, the rich food, and the other trappings of the American way of life. By zeroing in on the things that were added by the freaks we miss what they dropped. The recent interest in organic foods and handicrafts among larger and larger numbers of people demonstrates the many features of American culture that the revolution rejected and the kind of plain or natural products the idealists wish to put in their place.

The revolution in life-style had to come. It was inevitable that like all historical movements it would push the pendulum too far in the opposite direction. In the last few years the reaction had tended to moderate and we are even now witnessing the development of a new center for American culture which we will describe as an age beyond beauty and luxury: the age of the plain person.

CHAPTER 3
THE REACTION AGAINST BOTH CONFORMITY AND REVOLUTION

When the new mentality arose—around 1960—it appeared as a heterogeneous mass of individuals disturbed by the social situation around them as well as inspired by various teachings they had absorbed from their instructors and the books and plays that spoke to them of the project of becoming human. The earliest countercultural members were of vastly different types with a number of different interests, connected only by a sometimes unstated feeling that they must seek alternative pathways to their own maturity from the ones presented by the institutions of American society. The new mentality was a continuum running from the mystical and poetic on one end to those of political outlook who would in time become revolutionary in the militant sense of the term, on the opposite end.

In researching and writing *The New Mentality*,[1] and my later books on American culture,[2] I was very careful to point out that there were always two wings in Consciousness III, the active and the passive wings. I suggested in *A New Kind of Man*[3] that the passive life-style (popularly known as the hippie form) was probably not very fruitful if we were looking for ways in which to salvage our civilization, for it was an abdication of responsibility for others. I more or less gave an elegy over the grave of the active life-style (the way of the protestor), since by 1972 the political thrust of the new mentality was almost nil. I see this erosion of the active life-style as a great loss since political interest on the part of any group is the expression of the moral sense; in Christian terms, of concern for our fellowmen. The rejection and repression of the political wing of the new mentality by the sharp turn to the right in American society, beginning around 1967, dealt a harmful blow to the future progress of our society, in my opinion. We will probably see the negative effects of this as the years go by. In all events, while the passive or hippie life-style was and is severely criticized, the concentration of reaction against the political wing of the younger culture had the effect of tolerating and even of encouraging the growth of a passive style of life. The weight of society falling on the left side of the continuum of the counterculture had the effect of pushing young people and their allies into the passive wing. The internal developments within the passive wing, constantly shifting and working, since 1968, have now given form to our present cultural situation, which might be called the new naturalism, or the era of simplicity and plainness. Let me explain what I mean.

There is a great amount of vitality and intelligence in the straight or mainline American culture. Despite the fact that social surveys demonstrate a rather severe crisis of credibility concerning many social institutions, over the whole, there is an admirable elasticity that allows the culture to absorb widely divergent elements into itself. This ability to co-opt or absorb the passive wing of the new mentality has been demonstrated from the beginnings of the revolution in life-styles. It is the accommodation of the mainstream culture to the less threatening elements in the counterculture that has produced our present situation. In many respects this a good thing for the majority of people, although, like most compromises, it has avoided the hard and necessary job of dealing with the implications of the cultural revolution. I would suggest that in time we will suffer because we have avoided dealing with the crisis of authority and the question as to just what is included in searching for human happiness on a society-wide scale. These are the precise problems which were raised in the middle 1960's by the new mentality.

Quietism: A Separate Peace

I probably don't have to document the spread of quietism, of a slowing down of the frenetic activity of the middle 1960's in the youth culture. After the Cambodia incursion and the explosions at Kent State and Jackson State, the steam went out of college protest. The peace movement continued to the end of the war but with smaller numbers and a reduced punch. It won a moral victory when President Johnson announced that he would not run for office again, but it still took over five years for the war to wind down. The activistic wing of the new mentality, in the main, wound down and chucked it in much earlier. Among the older activists, in graduate school or out of college, the bitterness remained—their minds were not changed, but as far as the chance of successful social action was concerned —they "hung it up."

To "hang it up" means, in the jargon of the day, to quit. There has been a lot of quitting going on in recent years. I don't know what to say about a society and a governmental administration that succeeds in making its most concerned younger members quit. I can't say anything good. Part of "hanging it up" is the present philosophy of freedom through desiring less of the comforts of our society.

Doing with Less to Live Better

For some years now, millions of Americans have been shaken into a state of inward recognition that troubles many of them. That recognition is the insight that underlies Alvin Toffler's bestseller, *Future Shock,* in brief, that our times are moving too fast for our comfort. Our nation seems to be shaping up into a society that most of us would never have guessed possible. We are disturbed and frightened by the hard-core of poverty and unemployment, the residual hatred of the mainline culture by neglected minority groups, and, above all, the shattered and poisoned earth, air, and water of the continent along with the poisoned political atmosphere symbolized by Watergate and the ITT scandal. The wholesome places we recall from our youth seem to have disappeared, concreted over by suburbs and parking lots. The face-to-face societies of small towns and rural areas have given way to the rude—and often dangerous—impersonality of the crowded city. Nothing seems stable anymore, even the widely worshiped dollar has lost much of its power. Does it really matter that we make many more dollars than we once did? Inflation has risen faster than most of our incomes. Vague pictures of Germans in the 1920's hauling wagon loads of Reichsmarks to purchase a loaf of bread begin to disturb our dreams. The carefully planned lives so many of us built up in the suburbs now seem to be anchored in quicksand or perched on an earthquake fault.

Little by little, we begin to notice an out-migration from the city and its well-paying jobs, and from the suburbs with their sterile and safe cultures. Like rats running down the hawser of a damaged ship, some of our fellows are now seen to be pulling out, chucking it, going away so as to get back to a simpler, a plainer and more wholesome style of life.

Just why and how men and women today are opting out of mainline American culture is the subject of this book. The attractiveness of a simpler, alternative life-style can be read out of the sense of uneasiness millions of us have over what our lives have become.

Examples of "Chucking It"

Sam Bowers was a successful ad agency executive before "chucking it" and moving to a plainer life in California. In recounting his adventures for *Advertising Age*,[4] Bowers warns all prospective "new pioneers" of the need for a radical shift in values and consciousness on the part of those who seek to escape the security and ego-support of the business world for a simpler life-style. The urge to "get ahead," to acquire more and more "things" must be chucked first if one is to free himself for a new life. Bowers has moved from senior vice president at Warwick and Legler to a small house in California which he has remodeled himself. He is happy with his new state, but feels that others may not be. There is a wide gap between the $1.99 a gallon wine he now drinks and the expense account lunches and mixed drinks of the Madison Avenue life-style. There is more to "chucking it" than exchanging a suit for dungarees and growing a beard. Yet Bowers thinks the rewards are worth it. He says he traded all his security for the opportunity to enjoy his own life, fully, here and now. In so doing he feels that he better fulfills himself and gets closer to nature and to people.

Another of "the new drop-outs," as they are sometimes called, is Bill Roome. Bill gave up a nineteen-year career in Wall Street, as a partner and vice president in Dominick and Dominick, for an old farmhouse and a job in a hardware store in rural Vermont. The Roomes, products of the best the Eastern Establishment has to offer, began to tire of "the good life" and longed for a less pressure filled, more folksy life-style. The Roomes' experience illustrates some of the problems that must be foreseen—and solved, before a successful reentry into the simpler life can be made. Bill sought out and found a house and a job in his chosen area —thus forestalling the awful crunch of running out of money and having no alternative but to return to the city and its jobs, which has plagued other prospective "new pioneers." The Roomes have now made the adjustment to their new life and enjoy the unpretentious friendliness of their small-town neighbors. Being accepted for what you are, rather than for what you do or what you have is refreshing to them.

Co-opting the Symbols of Protest

The strength of the popular, mainline American culture is the ability it has to absorb many divergent elements into itself and then to homogenize those elements into a safe blandness. This absorption strength of our culture is the same genius—or demonic power—that lies in the English language itself. English is the one tongue in all the world that has absorbed words and terms from every language and culture in the world and has made them its own. American English and American culture have gone much further than the parent tongue and even the British Empire in their sponge-like properties. People from a hundred corners of the earth settled in this culture—bringing skins of black and white, brown and yellow to add to red, and produced the Howard Johnson motel.

The co-option of the counterculture's exterior signs is almost complete. Longer hair is seen on a majority of men. Moustaches, sideburns, and beards are common. Colorful clothes, even "far-out" styles, pour from the men's clothiers. The music and jewelry of the hippie adorn millions. The "straight" culture has even adopted the countercultural use of marijuana, making the misuse of this much maligned substance more widespread than it could ever be if it were limited to the young. What, after all, was the Vietnam experience of the military services but the counterculturalization of the army and navy?

Even the language of the counterculture has been adopted by wide segments of the mainline culture. The language of alienation—traditionally called cursing—has become the standard language of the school, university, and business. The slang of the street culture has passed into common parlance, and with language, much of the ethical outlook and alienation of the people who devised it. Co-option works both ways and the absorption of the counterculture by the mainstream has meant at least the partial absorption of the mainstream by the new mentality. Opposites do pass into each other, in life as in philosophy. A kind of rejection of traditional social conformity in dress, speech, outlook, life-style, and motivation has spread over the land. Now the new mentality, shorn of much of its ethical edge because its moral outrage has cooled, has spread in diluted form over the entire landscape.

Just attending church or a football game, or walking on the street today demonstrates the all pervasive spread of countercultural styles of appearance and dress—and the toning down of their original rejective meaning to "fads." "Message" tee shirts are worn by all ages; dungarees are worn on every kind of occasion, at least by many, and the majority of males wear longer hair than was the case ten years ago. Men's fashions have become precisely that, fashions that change in some particulars every year, and they now exhibit bright colors and fancy trimmings that have not been seen on men for two hundred years. I believe that as people have become convinced that they no longer can affect the course of political and social events (because of the huge, hidden power of great corporations and the nonresponsiveness of the government to their wishes) that they have turned toward the modification of their dress and lifestyles as a source of freedom and fulfillment. On this view, wearing either "skuzzy" or "fancy" clothes stems from the same motivation as does the seeking of a plainer form of life.

Quietism as the Inward Search

The landscape around us still contains much that is humanly foolish and dehumanizing, yet the vista we now turn to is the inscape of our own personalities. Many more of us than Carlos Castaneda have turned toward the journey to Ixtlan, the quest for the inner world.

The turn to the inscape has been heavily identified with drugs, but this is neither a fair nor an accurate judgment. The identification of drug experimentation with the search for self is an adolescent judgment based on the first, innocent turn-on to drugs in hippie communities in the early 1960's, as well as on the propaganda of drug recommenders like Timothy Leary. Such an easy identification overlooks the much older use of drugs by Aldous Huxley as well as the millennia-old practice of mysticism and the disciplines of the spiritual life.

The exploration of the inner world was always a part of the counterculture. From the beginning, men and women sought to get into contact with other parts of themselves beyond the surface conscious level. But this exploration was never limited to drug experimentation. The new mentality arose in a context of meditation, conversation, tramping in the mountains, prayer, the exercises of yoga and Zen. After all, why did we try to establish a new culture? Only the confused could ever have thought it was to create a cover for self-indulgence. Only the ill could have thought it was to encourage the murder of the self by damaging drugs. Only the hopelessly incapable of change could have identified the custom of using the mild marijuana plant with drug addiction.

Today the quest for the essential self is a theme of the new asceticism or age of plainness, the quietism that has resulted from the mutual co-option of the counter and mainline cultures. This quest is pursued along many lines, from diet to travel to music to reading to ecological consciousness. The self, even in its inwardness, is not found along one line alone. Millions now participate in various ways in a panmysticism that might bring a smile to Teilhard de Chardin.

Carlos Castaneda did not burst upon the countercultural scene until rather late, but when he did, he summed up, in his own person and work much of the passion and interest of the new mentality. Castaneda represents a turning away from science, the comforts of civilization and an attention to nature, the past and the inner world in a striking synthesis. To put it simply, he is a social scientist who became, after a ten-year apprenticeship, a sorcerer or medicine man. No other life history, even the move of Timothy Leary from university scientist to convicted drug offender, more graphically illustrates the trends of the counterculture than Castaneda.

Carlos Castaneda was born in Peru some forty-five years ago where he attended school before coming to the United

States to attend the University of California at Los Angeles. He was interested in studying anthropology and set out in the summer of 1960 to do field work on the Indian use of medicinal plants. This excursion led him into a realtionship with an old *brujo* or sorcerer, a Yaqui Indian named Juan Matus. Don Juan changed Castaneda's way of looking at the world and led him, after ten years, into the sorcerer's very different state of consciousness.

However, Carlos had not really grasped what Don Juan—representative of the wisdom of the past, a living link to the so-called primitive cultures—had tried to teach him. Carlos had thought that the use of drugs was necessary to have the sorcerer's eerie experiences. In 1971, he found out differently.[5] Castaneda records his reeducation about sorcery in *Journey to Ixtlan*.[6] This book is a valuable corrective to the widespread belief that only drugs can turn you on, drop you out, and tune you in to the essential self and the wonders of the whole creation. Castaneda symbolizes the whole quest for the plain person, to see the everyday, ordinary world with opened eyes, to look within and to find the macrocosmos in the microcosmos of the self.

Castaneda's three books are beautifully written and fascinating in the honest, not the press agent's sense, of that word. The respect they show for the Amerindian culture, which the white race almost totally destroyed, is as moving as it is healthy. The teachings of Don Juan do contain much wisdom, offering many freedoms, but also many fears. However, Carlos' shift of consciousness to membership (the word he uses) in another reality is the ultimate in quietism or "dropping out." He shrugs off, finally, not only the need for the creature comforts of Western civilization, but the whole mind-set of perceptions and interpretations that form the common psychic as well as social world of our culture. I have no philosophic quarrel with Don Juan's teaching that our "public world" is a description of reality rather than reality itself (that is, after all, what we learn from atomic physics), but I do have an ethical problem with the abandonment of our fellowmen in the midst of their trials in this particular view of reality. I cannot quarrel so much with the philosophic underpinning of Carlos' thought any more than I can help feeling that he rejects too much. Western ethics, based on Judeo-Christianity, has a concern for the fellow-man that is lacking in Don Juan's system.

A more intense critique must be made of Timothy Leary's drug cult. The selfishness of his stress upon personal sensual enjoyment is a key to his abandonment of ethics. Leary's insistence upon drug use also denies the natural human ability to rise to other or higher states of consciousness by meditation, prayer, and sacrifice. In all events, the use of a complex chemical like LSD-25 is hardly to be identified with being "natural" and living the simple life. Like Hugh Hefner's *Playboy* philosophy, Leary's drug philosophy is not natural or simple, but a perversion of the supersophistication of a technological age.

It would be difficult, if not impossible, to defend Leary's recommendations that we stayed "stoned" (drug intoxicated) as a counsel to adopt a simpler, more natural style of life. While the natural life undoubtedly has many "natural" highs in it, these are not generally induced by drugs. "The plain people" of all ages have usually been sober people who preach temperance rather than groups who undergo altered states of consciousness by means of chemicals. "Primitive" tribes in South America, Asia, and the Pacific areas do use various alcoholic concoctions and some tribes make use of the coca plant or even the opium-bearing poppy, but these are, in general, used for ceremonial purposes—or, as in the case of Peruvian Indians—to assist people laboring at high altitudes. In North America—to make the point simply—drugs and alcohol are very expensive and are either illegal or regulated by law. The person who desires to free himself from the shackles of the system will soon find it necessary to "give up" dependence upon substances that cost so much—and that put him so squarely under the eyes of the law.

There is a deeper reason why drug use is antithetical to living a plain life. That is the fact that many of the altered states of consciousness are not "natural" in any commonly accepted sense. Nightmares and high states of ecstasy are parts of every life, but these states are rare and come of themselves rather than being induced by various forms of intoxication.

It is my observation that the average person who attempts to modify his life-style toward a plainer way had better consider the detrimental effects of drugs and/or liquor. California wine and beer the body and the budget can handle, but anything else is really part of the escape mechanism of people still embedded in the Establishment culture. Everyone from the Hare Krishna freaks to the Jesus people to the new pioneers will bear witness to this insight.

Drugless High

The plain person today, for the most part, is one who rejects all use of psychotropic substances. Perhaps some use of marijuana can be found among the younger set seeking the simple life, but harder drugs ("chemicals" and "body drugs" such as "smack" or heroin) are put aside. On communes, such as Twin Oaks in Virginia,[7] men and women have tried to develop the microcosm, to experience a wider reality and taste human happiness by shifts in their behavior toward others. Twin Oaks has followed the thinking of B. F. Skinner as expressed in his book, *Walden II*,[8] while other communal experiments have followed more mystical or religious ideals. In both approaches there is an emphasis upon the natural, which means the ordinary world of experience, not some state induced by drugs. Carlos Castaneda, B. F. Skinner, and the Jesus people, all agree on that one central point.

Materialism, No, Spirituality, Si!

The very presence of ideals of plainness or naturalness in an advanced, complex technological society like ours implies some discomfort with materialism on the part of some of the population. Materialism is not necessarily completely rejected, indeed it probably cannot be wholly rejected, but its ultimacy for life's meaning is questioned when we idealize the plain life. For purposes, we will say that materialism is an uncritical acceptance of our present status in society and the world while spirituality implies a longing for—and an actual though fragmentary experience of—some transcendence over our place in space and time. Such searching for, and the finding of, various forms of transcendence characterizes the past few years in America and forms the basis for the new upsurge in spirituality that goes on all about us. The various aspects of this new spirituality are seen in the Jesus movement, the glossolalia or neopentecostal movement, interest in faith healing, and the Hare Krishna and other Eastern religious movements that are prospering in our culture.

This new spirituality is but an aspect of the centering upon the microcosm within the person that is now seen to be of supreme value. In some people it may be a mild interest in poetry or music, in others it may be the embracing of a new asceticism, such as the harsh disciplines of the Hare Krishna monastery. I have often thought that men and women today turn toward variants of the Eastern faiths for disciplines to aid them in spirituality because they were not challenged enough by their Christian congregations. Modern Christianity has not demanded very much of people, so consequently they have not valued it very much. The church may have sold its faith and disciplines too cheaply to satisfy the human urge to find the self.

People today seek for the inner discipline that will help them break free of materialism in the direction of a greater spirituality. In this search, Hinduism, Buddhism, Christianity, and occultism are utilized. Men and women wish to find a model on which to shape and fashion their lives. The various humanistic psychologies are pressed into service as auxiliary religious outlets. We find many persons seeking to find the way within by exploring the surface of the body. What the desire for a new naturalism looks for in a model surely includes feeling, as a counterweight to the insensitivity of modern society, a commitment to process in opposition to the fixed response, a strenuous or activistic life style as a reaction against the "cool," "don't get excited" philosophy that is so much in vogue now. Such a model would be responsive to the flux of life, knowing that change is inevitable and that we must find our peace within the changes, not outside them. Our model life-style would be pluralistic, accepting the divergences of beliefs and behaviors in our world without becoming lost in relativities. It would also be polyphonic, open to all experience, not locked into a one-dimensional vision of reality or a flat scientism. Above all, feeling will be stressed in our life-style model, but feeling in the sense of Alfred North Whitehead's unity of knowledge, not sensation alone.

It is this search for a total unity of knowledge and feeling that propels many people into occultic practices. Like Carlos Castaneda we are searching for an "old wisdom" that cuts below the many dimensions into which the modern world has split us.

The Search for Wisdom

The rejection of mainline society by the counterculture is more than a reaction against conformity in dress, speech, outlook, life-style, and motivation. It is a positive turning toward a life-style that grows out of wisdom rather than technological manipulation. Traveling around this continent I keep hearing expressions like these: "Where is the wisdom we have lost in quick retrieval data systems? Where, O IBM, where did we go wrong?" and, "I cannot change the ultimate futility of the human experience, but I can change the immediate frustration, fear, anger, sorrow and suffering of the people I meet." Such expressions are more than graffitti. They are expressions of a humane, cultured, highly intelligent philosophy—the sobered philosophy of the new mentality, of the simplicity offering counterculture in the middle 1970's. To criticize the homogenized, Howard Johnson, Holiday Inn, frozen foods, identical rooms civilization we now inhabit is not foolish carping. Too many times we have seen the buildings raised to plastic perfection, the freezers stocked with plastic foods, locked into plastic routines—and the sensitive among us have watched the human spirit depart.

When we can discuss the logical order of society and economics, the dynamics of social process and the changes in the weather, without responding as persons to the elegance and the beauty of that order, then we are split, even shattered, persons. We are split away from the instinctual ground of feelings within us and are mentally free-floating in the rationative functions of our own minds. The plain person seeks to pull himself together, to get back into touch with the creative ground—in older language, with Nature. But what is the nature of Nature? What are the characteristics of the creative ground? It is easy to say "creative," and "nature," but the plain person seeks to fill these abstract concepts with life. The creative ground, the "natural," for the counterculture, is a reference to the processes of life.

Life's processes are those internal and external factors that make for the continual pumping of our hearts and for the eventual failure of hearts, which is part of the process, too. They are also those hearts that will go on pumping after ours stop, as well as the continual radiation of power from the sun. Life's processes are what keep the world going when we close our eyes in sleep, as they ran the world before we were born. They are the vitality sources of my life and of your life, simply life itself. The process is, simply, *what is,* the crude, basic, sheer happening of events without us and within us. Life's processes, particularly in their recurring patterns, are the ultimate structures to which we must vibrate and respond if we are to live and move and have our being in happiness and health. It is to these patterns and structures that the new naturalism seeks to respond, not just to the conventional patterns of society. For while the conventions of society turn and change, the processes of life remain, fixed in the rhythms of our pulses and the temperature of our blood. They lie beneath, behind, beyond, and before all human explanation and interpretation.

Thinking along these lines while camping in the high Cascades a few years ago, I wrote these lines—rather expressive of the new naturalism, I believe. It has the same present hopelessness inspired by a future hope, the same short-range pessimism provoked by a long-range optimism that we see throughout the counterculture.

> You have forgotten the truth about time.
> You have broken the cycle of work and rest.
> You have lit an imaginary sun and raped the night,
> Stealing away her healing powers.
> If your tomorrow is not good
> It will only be
> Because you robbed tomorrow
> Tonight for the sake of today.

For the counterculture of the plain person, Nature is the symbol that coalesces our inner awareness of the processes of life, through our sensitivity, morality, aesthetics, and religion. *The plain person may believe in simplicity but he is not simple.* He knows that Nature is both the womb of God and the workshop of the devil, the crucible of history and the cradle of degradation. It is just the process and man must simply be silent before it. Life gets lived. There is something rather than nothing. Why, we really can't say. That which is, is. It is the ground of our Being, the only real part of us, the God beyond God in Tillich's theological phrase. Beyond subject and object, beyond substance and accidents, beyond body and consciousness, it is form, idea, and Spirit. We cannot fathom it, and if we truly respond to it we will not try, since the only adequate response is to rejoice in it. The plain person feels the lost element of mystical participation that has dropped out of Western philosophy. He feels the shriveled cloud of mysticism that has dried up in most Western religion as a cloudburst of spiritual drink. The plain person knows, because he feels, that the proper response to the processes of life is to love, to weep, to run, to speak, to sing, and to sleep—and not to analyze. This is the human response, not just a religious one, the response of the total being of the whole man—the man of science, art, play, work, and religion.

I think it is because of the commitment of the person who desires a plainer life to respond to the actual processes of life, to the real God behind the idols of traditional theologies, that so many people today are turning away from the "expected thing" in their life careers. The message—or example—of Zen Buddhism is strangely attractive to thousands because it consists of a real response rather than a verbal response in logical propositions. Zen provocation is not teaching, but a kind of studied attempt to make you lose your temper, or your mind—that you may come to your senses.

The counterculture was always heavily into philosophy. The activists dug Mao and Marx, Lenin and Marcuse. The passive side dug Emerson and Thoreau, Herman Hesse, and Buddha. When you consider the communities that the new mentality put together in many cities, it is easy to believe that the best school of philosophy was often located at the opposite side of the city from the philosophy department. The philosophy of the plain person runs heavily to religion. His faith is a kind of cosmic trait, an understanding with the world that includes the knowledge that everything we know will ultimately prove to be insufficient. Yet it also includes the feeling that we will act on what we know—regardless—along with the courage to go down when the processes of life turn up quicksand where our knowledge said there would be solid rock. All is relative in the world except faith, hope, love, courage, wisdom, and the intentionality that says, "to be or not to be" and I will be and I will hope that other men and women will be and do and hope and love, too.

Jesus People

Most of the Jesus people I have met would qualify in many ways to be known as plain people—at least on the surface and in their quest for spirituality. Yet they seem to have a defective form of feelings that lacks a genuine concern for all of mankind and for all the processes of life. Their depth, and therefore their knowledge, seems to be lacking. They have named themselves correctly when they wear the badge that says "One-Way." Looking for spirituality they looked in a good direction, the Bible, but they fastened upon it (perhaps because of the teachers they listened to) with a literalism that denies the spiritual wholeness and openness they were searching for. Jesus is a real and genuine spiritual power still living in our world, but he is a power that opens up, frees, when rightly apprehended. The Jesus people, in the main, do not give me the impression that they have been freed. They rather seem to be locked into a story recorded in the Gospels, not active participants in a living power at work in the world now.

Until the Jesus people begin to recognize that Jesus is the Lord of all life, and that he communicates with us through the processes of life, as well as the Bible, they will live as split and fragmented an existence as the materialists in the mainline culture. They will continue to falsely worship Jesus as Lord only of a narrow circle of Bible-quoting, "evangelistic" activity and miss the many splendored revelation of the Lord of life in all life's dimensions. This false communion with Jesus Christ explains the egocentricity and narrowmindedness of many of the Jesus people. They have grabbed onto a security, a stability of a sort, for personal reasons—to keep off dope, liquor, or something else. They are looking for the father figure they missed in childhood, for the in-badges of a close-knit group they have never known. They do not seem to be seeking freedom to be human, freedom to experiment with life, freedom to love.

What's So Bad About Feeling Good?

The whole quest of Carlos Castaneda and Timothy Leary was to be happy, "to feel good." The counterculture, too, believes what Aristotle taught—that man, above all else, desires to be happy. In 1968, Mary Tyler Moore and George Peppard made a tragically funny comedy movie, called *What's So Bad About Feeling Good?* This situation piece showed us the cynicism and meanness of average people and introduced a strange "virus" carried by a toucan bird that made people feel happy. Once thousands of people were "infected" with this happiness bug, the usual state of society came to a halt. The government (read the Establishment) immediately gathered their forces to combat such a "subversive" virus. The point is well taken. If people were happy, really happy, much of what is the backbone of society—cigarettes, liquor, tranquilizers, psychiatry, police science—would not even be necessary. The counterculture rather firmly believes this and attempts to build parallel institutions in its communes and cooperatives.

The New Society by Experiment

The state of Vermont is full (in the summertime) of communal experiments. It seemed to me as I traveled there several summers, that every tenth farmhouse along Route 2 was a commune. The further north one drove, the more primitive the communes, until, at the Canadian border, a group of young people were spread out over a meadow, living in Boy Scout-like tepees made of branches. These people were looking for happiness through freedom from things. Unfortunately, there are a minimal number of "things" necessary for survival in a cold climate. Winter comes and destroys all but the most mature and organized of groups.

In Ohio, communes run to religious experiments for the most part. One, with which I am familiar, is located in the northwestern Ohio area below Toledo. This group consists of Catholic priests and lay people who felt called by the Holy Spirit to develop a more open, loving way of life. Leaving the regular parish, the lay people sold their homes and moved to the country, where the commune, in effect, lived off the proceeds of the sale of their former homes and cars. In time, they found the "natural work" they felt called to do, and proceeded to move to Bolivia. Apparently, they want to evangelize and help the peasants there.

Another Ohio commune specialized in baking organic bread. Here the desire for a natural diet, a strong element in the plain person culture, is dominant. These people have their own recipe for bread and it tastes delicious. However, they do not believe in the ordinances of man and thus have run into problems with the health authorities and police of a number of cities. They have been arrested for selling bread that was not inspected by the State Health Department, as well as for not having a vendor's license. This particular commune seems to be totally involved in the baking of bread, an act that has taken on a religious connotation for them. This rejection of interest in the ordinary affairs of the world and devotion to some "natural work" is the overriding characteristic of the age of the plain person.

Discovering Beauty and Sanity in the More Natural

A couple who did feel and answer the call of a simpler, harsh, yet natural life was Sue and Eliot Coleman. The Colemans' story was reported to the country in the July 13, 1971, issue of *The Wall Street Journal*. Sue and Eliot, with their small daughter, Melissa, purchased forty rough, tree-covered acres near the central coast of Maine. They now live in a one-room cabin which they built themselves, securing their drinking water from a stream that lies a quarter of a mile from their door. There is no electricity in their home, only the light given by kerosene lanterns. Among the many things they have "chucked" are telephones and televisions. Their only concession to the twentieth-century worldwide media network is a portable radio. Their major connection to modern technological life is the ownership of a truck and a jeep. The Colemans look forward to getting rid of the truck, and, eventually of chucking the jeep, too.

In 1970-71, the Colemans grew some 80 percent of their own food, requiring only $2,000 for additional food and farm and family expenses. Interestingly, $750 of those expenses went for the support of the truck and the jeep. How much freer of society's control one would be without a dependence on wheels! The Brazilians have a saying that aptly illustrates the tyranny of automobiles: "He who buys a car takes on a second family to feed." The Colemans and others of the "chuck-it" generation realize this very clearly.

Sue and Eliot were influenced in their adoption of the plain life by the famous pioneers of the new pioneering life style, Scott and Helen Nearing. The Nearings (Helen is 69, Scott is 89) made the move to the simple life in the early 1930's. At first they homesteaded in Vermont, and when it became too crowded, moved into Maine. In 1954, Scott and Helen wrote of their philosophy in *Living the Good Life*.[9] This book sold 10,000 copies in sixteen years, then in September 1970, a new edition appeared. Under the impact of the widespread interest in finding a more natural life, over 50,000 copies of the book were sold in nine months. Helen Nearing says she knows of over one hundred people in her central Maine area who have bought land and moved on it—to live in harmony with each other and the land.

Why Pioneers Move Out

The Nearings report that they made their move back to the land about forty years ago in order to find for themselves "simplicity, freedom from anxiety or tension, an opportunity to be useful and to live harmoniously." The pressures of modern life, the rush to acquire goods and services through wealth, all these chains and "tracks" were rejected by the Nearings in favor of "the good life." And, in what did that good life consist? In the production of the food one needs to live and in the surplus time left over to follow one's interests, hobbies, and avocations, including reading, writing, hiking, and talking with each other.

Other new pioneers have changed their life-styles because of what I would call "political fatigue" or "civic disgust." Such pioneers have "had it" with the corruption of governmental administration, and especially reject the arguments for war-like intervention in Indochina. David and Debbie Wilson, another "plain" family, reported, in David's words, "I don't want to earn a lot of money because I don't want to pay taxes to a government that's been lying about Vietnam and its intentions of solving social problems."[10]

Such disgust with social processes is not new, but formed the backbone of the yearning of Henry David Thoreau to find a cleaner life in harmony with nature. It is reported that Ralph Waldo Emerson passed by the town jail and observed that Thoreau was a prisoner there. "What, Mr. Thoreau, you in jail?" Emerson asked. And Thoreau replied, "What, Mr. Emerson, you are not in jail?" Thoreau couldn't understand how any moral man could stay out of jail in a state that upheld the fugitive slave laws. Disgust with social injustice was part of Thoreau's motivation to seek out the plainer, more moral life of noncompetition.

In the 1970's, there are a multitude of reasons for social disgust or political fatigue on the part of millions of Americans. The deterioration of the inner city, the demoralization of urban families, the stunning crime rate, the destructive drug traffic, all these elements of American society contribute to the psychic disgust and fatigue of many citizens. Built upon these rotting national foundations (and in many ways causes of the social rot, through "benign neglect") are the nationwide scandals of an improper war waged by the presidencies of a number of administrations that eventually destroyed the social fabric of several Asian nations and came close to destroying the democratic society of the United States.

There is a scripture that says, "Come out from them, and be separate from them, says the Lord (2 Cor. 6:17)." Consciously or unconsciously, thousands of Americans responded to that call during the Vietnam War and "silent majority" period. After the attempts to change public policy by ballot and demonstration failed (since the President would not listen), many youths moved to the country and the forest. The abandonment of career planning and of a desire to graduate or to prepare for future administrative level employment has been marked among American university students for some ten years. Among these psychically outraged students the new naturalism grew up and new pioneers were recruited. "Hell, no, we won't go" applies to the jobs that serve an oppressive social system as well as to overseas war. Like Lot's family, many student couples and young instructors and their families have fled from Sodom—both out of anger and from a fear that our society is in the process of destroying itself. The theme of self-destruction in the near future (unless we change things) is also very widely spread in our day.

The spread of the Jesus people among youth, the revival of fundamentalism across the country and the emergence of unusual sects all point to the apocalyptic expectation of the "end of the world" that grasps the imagination of millions. Hippie-type astrology freaks also predict tidal waves, earthquakes, and falling stars. And all this points to the deep fear in millions that our culture has become so corrupt that God or nature or history or its own social contradictions will shortly destroy it.

A New-old Life-style

The multitudes who seek a more natural style of life today probably fasten upon its ancientness, its traditional quality, more than anything else. The plainer life of the new pioneer is the readoption of an abandoned life-style—a way of living that once was followed by the majority of Americans on farms and in small towns. Yet, it is impossible to go backward, we cannot go "home" again. To resurrect the past in any fashion is actually to create a different future, that is, to make something new patterned on our memories of the past.

The Colemans' experience on forty Maine acres illustrates the new-oldness of the modern pioneer movement. The Colemans raised much of their own food, but a number of items had to be purchased from modern stores. They like peanut butter and honey and use cooking oil—and they find those items difficult to produce themselves. The Colemans purchased such foods, although it is true that a big enough farm operation could produce peanut butter from its own peanuts, oil from its own cotton seed or soybeans, and honey from its own hives.

The Colemans also have kept one foot in the twentieth-century technological culture by utilizing a portable radio, a truck, and a jeep. These possessions do embarrass them and they look forward to selling the truck and eventually the jeep. But even if the Colemans were to chuck out every modern machine, their life-style would not be and could not be anything more than a new-old life-style. The very basic matter of their knowledge of nutritional requirements—a factor of much importance to most new pioneers—puts these people on a different scientific plane from even the farmers of the late nineteenth century. Not many generations ago men and women thought of the tomato as an ornamental plant with possibly poison fruit. It was a brave person who first ate a tomato! No, the knowledge of necessary vitamins and minerals that the new pioneers possess, and which forms a large part of the "creed" of the plain person movement, is a sure sign of the modernity of this life-style. Another, more basic consideration relates to the reason as to why one might live simply in the wilderness. The old-fashioned pioneer was looking for a new start. He suffered and lived a plain existence (for the most part) so that he could rise by hard work and "luck" to something better. Indeed, most of the middle class are the descendants of pioneers and farmers like that. The nineteenth-century plain person was upwardly mobile whereas the twentieth-century plain person is deliberately downwardly mobile. For this reason the two life-styles (nineteenth and twentieth centuries) have a major difference with regard to invention. The older pioneers were invention-prone and actively sought to produce more efficient technologies. The new pioneers have deliberately turned their back on efficient technology and seek "inventions" that allow them to return to a muscle-power society. The face of the new pioneer, already marked by the anxiety and pollution of a modern technological society, is turned determinedly toward the past. I submit that this turning away is a new-old life-style.

The Place You Must Be to Turn Away

There is a very real sense in which the new pioneering life-style was not possible for most people until a high peak of affluence was reached by the majority of American citizens. In order to turn your back on present-day technology with its comforts and securities, you must have reached a place where you have enjoyed technology's good things as well as suffered its demonic nature. It is remarkable, but we do not see poor white people embracing the plain life (indeed, they want to escape it) nor do we see Blacks or Chicanos or American Indians adopting (willingly) the style of the new pioneers. These groups have not yet reached the apex of American technological culture and enjoyed its rewards. Minority people do not yet have a surfeit of what the American economy can give. For the most part, the embracers of the plain life have turned their backs on the modern world from a place near the pinnacle of power and comfort. Like the hippie and beat generational movements, the plain life is an outgrowth of the plenty of the North American middle class. As attractive as much of the plain philosophy is, it remains true that the idea of doing without things becomes a desirable objective only among people who have been surrounded by and stuffed full of things all their lives. "Doing without" is a unique experience for the sons and daughters of the middle and upper classes. It isn't anything new—or desirable—to the children of the poor. *Sic transit gloria mundi.*

Values Within the Very Human

Just because the plain life has its origins in the overaffluence and world-weariness of the middle and upper classes does not mean that it does not have real values to give us all. The origin of a movement is irrelevant when we consider the truth and/or helpfulness of its doctrines and examples. The plain life must be judged on its own merits, not on the demerits of the upper social classes.

CHAPTER 4
TWO CULTURES
IN COLLISION

One might wonder why we are concerned about two cultures in a work on the new life-style that aims to free itself from the mainline culture. There is a good reason, for new life-styles only come into being out of conflict and because of deep social need. It is because of the contradictions within each of us and within our society that the experiments in plain living are now going on. Even the Amish, whom we will discuss in this chapter, evolved their particular way of life out of conflict and rejection of their society. Only as we understand the plight which our fellowmen throughout the society are in will we understand our own problems, just as only through a full acknowledgment of our own problems will we learn to love our fellowmen, and perhaps find the strength to build a new life.

There is a mixture of motives in American society today. There are many elements that pull each of us in many directions. Indeed, each person of us is a battleground in which two cultures are in collision. We are, in the main, not "whole" people in the sense of a unity of consciousness and physical activity. The overwhelming influence of the mass media has spread ideals and ideas of both the more conservative dominant culture and the liberal-radical ideals of the counterculture. We thus hold mixed motives and often pursue contradictory goals. Reaction and revolutionary ideas, along with the new naturalism's rejection of both goals, mingle in the minds of millions today. Such split goals produce an uncomfortable feeling in us, but this spiritual discomfort is one of the conditions of human growth. Closed minds, conservative or radical, are not able to grow but experience only pain without spiritual gain.

Contradictory Goals

In America the population is split into different segments on each of the several issues that agitate the country. We are, in general, both for increased industrial wealth and for ecological salvage and renewal. The advent of economic inflation and the devaluation of the dollar disturbs everyone, yet an increasing number are drawn to the "greening" or back-to-the-land syndrome. We are both for more money and against more materialism. We long to improve our physical lot and to explore the depths of our souls. Some hard-nosed economists have put the problem bluntly, we must decide how much ecological damage we are willing to accept as the price for a high standard of living. We must also decide how much we are willing to pay in increased prices for the restoration of the land, air, and water that are degraded by industrial processes. It is not at all clear that the answer to environmental pollution lies in the recommendation of a plain person style of life for everyone. We have reached a population size, worldwide, such that we could not hope to feed, house, and clothe these billions of people on a simpler, rural type of economy. Nevertheless, *the call for a simpler lifestyle that has fewer expectations is necessary if we are to continue in an acceptable economic condition without destroying the life-support system of the planet.*

Journeying to the Future by Way of the Past

Carlos Castaneda found that making a breakthrough to the spiritual world of the occult made him frightened and unhappy. In the words of his sorcerer-teacher, Don Juan, he stood between the world of everyday reality and the world of the sorcerer, no longer a native of ordinary reality and fearful of being lost in the sorcerer's world. He found that the life of the occultist becomes a journey without end. Many of us are like Carlos in some respect. We are caught between two modes of consciousness, not yet a full participant in the new mentality and no longer completely integrated in the old. For us the myths of Consciousness I and II are broken and the myths of Consciousness III are, as yet, undeveloped. We hang between, as Alexander Pope remarked about the men of his transitional generation, in doubt to act or rest. We still equate ugliness and a lack of harmonious physical attributes with loneliness, while striving to reduce all human appearance to unity by a movement toward plainness—even to the ultimate plainness of the unisex look.

Yet, it could be that this confusion, this "sticking" between two worlds is the best place we can be. Perhaps here, in this middle position, we can find a spiritual depth beyond the carping of the counterculture and the defensiveness of the conservatives. May it be that we are being forced to join together what is good from both the mainline and the counterculture into a new spirituality?

Order out of Disorder

The desire today to open a new life-style for oneself grows out of a wish to create order for oneself out of the disorder of a disturbed self in a troubled country in a chaotic time. The foundation for the dis-ease one feels is both social fatigue and the achievement of some social and financial success within the disturbed organism of society. The depths of the spiritual crisis men and women feel in the late twentieth century is revealed by their idealization of an adoption (in more and more cases) of a style of life that was perfected by the strangest sectarians in the past. To better understand this, it would be well to describe the life-style of the original "plain people," the Amish.

The Plain People

The Amish are famous for their appearance and "difference" throughout American society, although they are found (for the most part) only in Pennsylvania, Ohio, Wisconsin, Indiana, and Iowa. Their numbers are not large, running to perhaps 50,000 members and a slightly larger number of children. The typical Amishman dresses plainly, in black suits and wide-brimmed hats, so far rejecting social fashion that he does not even have buttons on his clothes. By religious conviction and personal interest the Amish live in seclusion, withdrawn from the affairs of the world. We ordinary citizens are really aware of the Amish because their efforts not to change at all bring them into conflict with the laws of the state.

Fundamentally, the Amish are religious sectarians whose "church" arose out of the Left Wing of the Protestant Reformation in the sixteenth century. The religious stream out of which they emerged is the Mennonite tradition. The basis of their faith is the Schleitheim Confession of Faith of 1527 and the Dortrecht Confession of Faith of 1632. Basically, the Mennonite view centers on voluntary church membership, adult baptism, refusal to bear arms as soldiers or policemen, refusal to participate in government (local or national), closed communion and footwashing, refusal to take an oath, separation of believers from nonbelievers (including other Christians), expulsion (excommunication) of unfaithful members, mutual aid among members, and local ordination of church leaders.

The Amish share these beliefs with the other Mennonite bodies, but separated from fellow "plain people" in 1693-97 under the leadership of Jakob Ammann over strict use of the Ban, or the expulsion of nonfaithful members. In German, the language of the Swiss and South German lands where the Mennonites lived, the Ban is called the *Meidung*. It means not only an ecclesiastical decision but the strict shunning of anyone out of favor with the group. Ammann thought the groups in his day were lax on banning, and fought for strict shunning as a guard against change. The congregations who agreed with him were called (later) "The Amish."[1]

In the eighteenth century, the Amish migrated to America, settling in Pennsylvania. After a time almost all the Amish congregations moved to the New World, the few remaining in Europe being absorbed by other Mennonite groups. Prospering in Pennsylvania, over the past two hundred years, the Amish have spread out over the Midwest and into Ontario.

Life-style

Basically, the Amish are interesting to us today because of their life-style, which is one of rejection of progress and of a feeling of unity with one another and with the land. The Amish are reminders that one can live without luxuries and comforts, even in America. It is possible to keep clear of the trap of "planned obsolescence," although John A. Hostetler[2] and William I. Schreiber[3] both point out the subtle influence of American economics on the Amish.[4] Because horse-drawn equipment is no longer manufactured, the Amish now use mechanical farm machinery, although they reject central heating, running water, and flashy cars.

The attraction of the Amish to the "new pioneer" spirit in many Americans really rests on the achievement by the group of a plain, simple life that is good, nourishing, and conducive to quiet happiness in many. Their simple life consists of farming—or farm-related occupations—wearing simple clothes that are the same for children and adults, riding in horse-drawn buggies, and living in large, white-painted farmhouses. A museum and exhibit of Amish life called Rockome Gardens, near Arcola, Illinois, draws thousands of visitors every year. Nearby, on the Kaskaskia River, there is a reconstructed nineteenth-century community called "Old Bagdad" that also is popular.

Amish life, as distinct from religious belief, may be said to revolve around three principles, the family, the community, and the means of life. These three principles are not different in essence from those of primitive, tribal people in many times and places.

The family is basic to Amish life, as it is to a plain life anywhere. The Amish have large families since they do not practice birth control. A related Anabaptist group, the Hutterites, has the highest birth rate in North America. The Amish have a high rate of population increase, too. Children are completely integrated into family life, taking part in the family's work as soon as they are able to help. Youngsters are allowed to attend school only through the eighth grade, many times attending schools directed by the community. This refusal to send their children to high school often brings Amish parents into conflict with local and state school authorities. The Amish are not against learning as such, only against "worldly" learning. It is reported that the Amish sent one of their number around the world in order to check on the rumor that the world was round and not flat. When he returned and said the world was indeed round, the Amish stopped teaching that it was flat!

The family is built up and the community increased by the marriage of Amish young people, who start out at home or on a rented property and work themselves up to ownership of their own farms. Through this "plowing back" of their own offspring, Amish communities steadily grow in numbers and in wealth. Interestingly, while there is much mutual aid, there is no communism involved in this way of life. Individualism and initiative are both respected.

The family is the basis of the community which is a very real "extended family." Each Amish "church" is really a "church district" consisting of the Amish families which live in a general area. Such a "church district" may include from twenty-five to two hundred families, the number being determined by how many people can be accommodated in the house or barn of any one of their members. Worship services are held every other Sunday within homes as there is no church building. Communion is held twice a year, but only after every church member has resubscribed to the current "rules and regulations."

While the family is the real basis of Amish life, the community does provide support, protection from the world and help in time of trouble. No Amishman will accept welfare, social security, or other outside help. The community takes care of its own. An Amish "barn-raising," when hundreds of people come to help one member put up a new barn, is famous in Pennsylvania. The closeness of face-to-face contacts, complete acceptance and trust in an Amish community makes their way of life very appealing. In a day when the street crime in American cities is so bad that we fear to walk outside after dark, the atmosphere of peace and acceptance in an Amish community exercises a strong attraction—with good reason.

The means of life—or the instruments of production and the means of earning a living—among the Amish turn squarely around land. William I. Schreiber reports the experience of Preacher Eli J. Miller, who died at age 74 after building up his private estate from a small, rented farm to a 160-acre farm that he owned outright. This is the desired course of life for every Amishman. The land is loved and well-cared for, although Hostetler tells us that the Amish do not accept the modern practice of contour farming and strip plowing taught by the state universities. Above all, the Amish believe in feeding the soil, especially with barnyard manure. They are evidently successful in their land treatment since their farms are famous for productivity. Despite the Amish rejection of the "world," meaning human society—and especially the city—the physical world is thought to be good and not corrupting. While Amish families will not attend the theater, they will go to the zoo to see the animals. The hard work, thrift, and cooperation demanded by rural living are valued by the Amish because in such a relationship to nature it is felt that God can be experienced.

The land and its care, the increase of the family and the flocks, the singing of hymns and the study of the Bible, these are the activities of the Amish community, year in and year out. Although it does change, the group changes only very slowly and the community remains bound together in a multitude of ways, both real and symbolic.

One of the favorite Amish pastimes is visiting. Visiting

friends and relatives may take the form of long journeys from one settlement to another. Conversation, that forgotten art in modern American life, flourishes among them, in Pennsylvania Dutch, or the low German spoken by all Palatinate peoples in the seventeenth century, as well as in English. The Amish also have at least a passive knowledge of high (formal) German as the sermons and scriptures are all presented in German.

Above all, the Amish families help each other. They feel no need for insurance or government aid because the community closes ranks to help whenever there is sickness, death, or a fire. This is not a community of goods, such as the Hutterites have, but a genuine sharing of one's own goods, money, and time out of a serious concern for another member of "the household of faith." In a time of a real lack of social cohesion in America, this community of concern looks very inviting to many. We "English" (non-Amish) people would like to build such a community, too.

The Contradictions Within Us Are the Source of Our Pain

Over and over representatives of both the mainline culture and of the counterculture call out for the sanctity of the individual, yet both sides stress conformity to some group at the same time. We long to exhibit our individual distinctiveness but are fascinated by the demands of the nation, of our in-groups or our commune upon us. We even consider turning marriage into a larger group affair. Do we really know what we want?

It should be no surprise to us to find that we are confused as to the goals we wish to reach. Our lifetime has been one of depression, recession, high employment, unemployment, affluence, hard times, war, cold war, and uneasy peace. Our lifetimes have shared in the Dickensian best of times and worst of times in large measure. We do sense our need of more community and, at the same time, for more privacy, very keenly. Without doubt, we need both, and the problem is, what measure of both is needed for mental and spiritual health?

Ours seems a time when our awareness of human needs and problems has outrun our ability to work up the moral energy to attempt to meet those needs and solve those problems. Our huge population, too, is not of one mind on all issues, either. The fundamental fact about North American society is its diversity, not its uniformity—something we often forget. I have tried to point out this diversity in *The Recovery of America*.[5] Michael Novak makes the political point clear in his *The Rise of the Unmeltable Ethnics*.[6]

Perhaps it is too easy, too smooth to say we have two cultures in America. We definitely have two, but the question remains as to whether we don't have a good many more. Women's liberation, civil rights organizations, peace movements, ethnic movements of several kinds, as well as homosexual movements function in our society side by side with ultraconservative religious and political organizations. What one side affirms, another denies. In point of fact, few citizens give unquestioned loyalty to any one of these groups. Most of us are a little frightened by them, and more than a little confused. The rising of the American Indians at Wounded Knee, South Dakota, is a case in point.

When the organism is frightened, confused, made anxious, it may be expected to retreat, to withdraw, to turn within. A very great amount of the momentum toward a plainer form of culture, with its attention focused on private issues, is just such a withdrawal from our confusing social world.

The movie *Billy Jack*, which turns around the character of an American Indian recently released from war service, points up the confusion inherent in the countercultural personality—as well as in the "straight" personality. Billy Jack identifies with a Quaker, pacifistic teacher who operates a free type school for children in the countryside of a Western state. This school represents a kind of liberal ideal of integration, arts and crafts, inner freedom, and peace among Blacks, Whites, and Reds. But when "redneck" reactionaries trouble the school, Billy Jack reverts to his military outlook and abandons the way of peace. He beats a gang of toughs into submission when they assault some young people in town. Later, when trouble comes to the school, Billy Jack goes to earth in a church building and carries on a firefight with everyone, including the police. Can you defend peace with firearms? What constitutes capitulation to the powers of evil? Billy Jack is eventually induced to surrender, but as he is driven away in a police car, the roadside is lined with youngsters who silently raise their clenched fists in the sign of revolution. Confused? Yes, we are confused, from left to right in America, with the greatest confusion, it seems to me, concentrated in the center. Do we need to destroy—or abandon—our society in order to save it?

Apart from a spiritual commitment, it does not seem possible to me for anyone, or any group, "to know their own mind." Goals are not things in themselves but stem from a vision of what things might be if what we believe was brought into the reality of altered social relations. Men work for a goal only to enhance the reality of their articles of faith. If we have no such faith, then we have no goals.

It seems that we must continually crucify ourselves as long as we do not plumb the depths of our spirits to seek out the articles of our faith. One form of withdrawal: meditation, prayer and reflection, may be a very necessary, nonescapist, mode of being for all of us right now.

Religion in a Blighted Aquarian Aspect

Ours is a land of churches. They are everywhere. Although we may be experiencing some loss of membership in the mainline churches today, they are still very much alive and socially powerful. Religion, too, as an aspect of human personality, is deeply relevant to most North Americans, including millions with no communion membership at all. The religions of the East and the paths of the occult are growing. The Jesus movement's signs and Bible-talk are to be found everywhere. Yet, religion, organized and unorganized, seems as goal-confused as any other social institution. If you look for a clear "yes" or "no" on any issue, you would do well not to look to the average church. Just here is a large part of the North American schizoid experience.

The religious scene in America is clearly in some sort of retreat from the social involvement that characterized the churches in the 1960's. The trend toward greater social quietism is unmistakable in all denominations. Perhaps people have substituted the traditional, socially quiet and privatistic goal of immortality for the achievement of more elements of the kingdom of God on earth.

The schizoid society is best seen in the desire we have (all of us) to live with as many luxuries and as little work as possible. We want to be religious in a general sense, but reject the specific and central teachings of Christianity. What a contrast with the Amish!

Dean M. Kelley has made the contradictions of American religious life abundantly clear in his book *Why Conservative Churches Are Growing*.[7] Briefly, Kelley offers statistical evidence in the form of graphs to show that the denominations that make up the National Council of Churches (the "more liberal and established" churches) are declining in membership, while the conservative bodies (such as the Southern Baptists, Missouri Synod Lutherans, Mormons, and Jehovah's Witnesses) are increasing. He then goes on to offer hypotheses to explain this phenomenon that will cheer the hearts of "conservatives" as much as they will chill the hearts of "moderates" and "liberals." Among his theses are the following:

1. The mainline churches are dying today because they are not very religious at all.[8]
2. Churches that try to be responsive to the needs of men and work cooperatively with other groups to meet these needs are following a recipe for failure.[9]
3. Modern men don't want a reasonable, tolerant, relevant church, but want, because they need, a church with absurd beliefs, unreasonable requirements, irrelevant preoccupations, and distinctions between those who belong and those who don't.[10]

4. But chiefly, the liberal churches are declining and the conservative ones growing because the business of religion is to explain the meaning of life in ultimate terms, and the liberal churches are not doing this while the conservatives are.[11]

Kelley goes on to develop the idea that the giving of meaning to life entails making heavy demands upon people, exacting a commitment to strict discipline and making a clear (even if intolerant) distinction between the insiders and outsiders. Indeed the unlovely characteristics that we mainline Christians do not appreciate in conservatives are precisely the marks (says Kelley) of someone who is fully in a meaning system. The exclusiveness, enthusiasm, even fanaticism of the sectarian is what it takes to build a strong church movement and to attract new members. Mr. Kelley may well be right in this hypothesis as it is supported by psychological evidence.

I do not for a moment want to dispute Kelley's point, that this inculcation of exclusiveness is the reason conservative groups grow. I think his evidence here is as sound as his statistics. I do, however, want to take severe exception to his suggestions that the mainline churches must adopt these same tactics or die. Indeed, Kelley holds that the decline in the Lutheran Church in America, United Presbyterian Church, Episcopal Church, and United Methodist Church (and others) is already such that these organizations must die anyway. While I don't interpret the statistics we have accumulated over the past few years that drastically, I don't have any way of disputing Kelley's opinion—only time will tell us how serious our illness is. I do say this, a church that would take all the steps suggested by Kelley (if it were possible for large, mainline churches to take them, and Kelley says it isn't, and I agree with him) in order to become a growing "church" would not be a Christian church. Note that I said all the steps suggested by Kelley. Some of them, I am convinced, are in accordance with a mature understanding of the gospel and ought to be part of the discipline of any Christian group. The conformity of the Amish experience to many of Kelley's strong points should be noted.

Let us review some of Kelley's hypotheses and suggestions and draw some theological distinctions between them.

1. Religion must give men a sense of meaning in life and when it doesn't it cannot hold or attract members. This is most certainly true. If trust and confidence in the love and wisdom of God as revealed in Christ do not give this meaning, there is little reason to believe it will be found elsewhere. Insofar as our preaching, teaching, and practices in any church do not convey this meaning, then we need to redouble our efforts to give men meaning in the midst of the world and its problems, not seek to flee into a corner in the sectarian mode.

2. Kelley says a strong religion will have goals, controls, and communication.[12] Undoubtedly, he is right. I take exception to his fixation on the sect as the ideal type of strong religion, however. Kelley stresses the fanatical elements in religion that have caused persecution, intolerance, crusades, prejudices, and wars for centuries. Again, psychologically, I think Kelley is right. The developing of these attitudes does build a strong group. But I do not believe it builds a Christian group. In fact, Kelley points out that adherents of such absolutistic groups could have another theology substituted for the one they follow and it would make no difference in their lives.[13]

I would suggest that this is the precise point where the true absolutism of the Christian gospel (and of a mature theology) differs from the assured results (which are absolutely correct) of statistics and of religious psychology and sociology. If we are to do anything to get and hold members, anything to give men meaning, then we are dealing not with the absolute truths claimed by the conservatives who are now "successful," but rather we have fallen into a relativism and pragmatism so extreme that it denies the gospel of Christ. There are some things one cannot do and still claim to be Christian.

3. Kelley observes that, "On the one hand, ultimate meaning is essential to human life, and is effective to the degree that it demands and secures a central commitment in men's lives." (This is theologically and psychologically true.) "Yet on the other hand, to attain that central significance, it often rides roughshod over other interests and values, sometimes even disregarding human well-being."[14] (This is certainly historically often true, but, to the degree that it is true, then that meaning is unchristian and must be resisted, not sought out by Christians.)

What is theologically missing from Kelley's hypotheses and evaluation is a recognition of the "radical evil" (Kant's phrase) in the world that the church calls original sin. Kelley's suggestions that churches can grow by exclusivism (which, practically speaking, they can) overlook Jesus' words, "If you love those who love you, what reward have you (Matt. 5:46)?"

4. Kelley observes that "the very qualities that make a religious movement objectionable to critical outsiders are what make it convincing to adherents and potential converts."[15] I think this is true, but I would suggest that the objectionable qualities of a genuine Christian movement will be its lack of pride and self-centeredness, its openness to all who are drawn to Christ, its persistent demonstration of lack of prejudice, lack of hatred and active solicitude for humanity in its struggle toward freedom, health, and fulfillment in a sin-enslaved world. This liberal (free) expression of love and concern will draw those whose hearts are open and will raise the ire of those who are entrapped in selfishness and pride. It has always been that way and it is now. I guess I am saying, straight out, that the human motivations that lead men to the strict, exclusive conservative "churches" are real and strong, but they are the characteristics of sinfulness. Mr. Kelley's presentation of statistics, psychology, and sociology is all in order, and makes sense, but so did Satan's temptation of Jesus. Just jump off the temple and draw a crowd. Jesus wouldn't accept that logic then and I don't think we should accept it now.

What the Plain Person Has to Tell the Churches

The person who has decided to chuck it and move to a smaller town or a farm in the woods might well tell both the right and the left wings of the church to forget it. In a way, the actions of the new pioneers speak louder than words, for it is clear that the church plays little or no part in their future plans. The new pioneering of farms and simpler lives, unlike many of the communes, does not often reveal a religious underpinning. I think that the silent message of the new plain people is a thunderous condemnation of the conservative churches who have stood by and let the social fabric fall to pieces—aiding and abetting its breakup by their moralism and support of "law and order" politicians like Nixon, Agnew, and Mitchell.

Much more to the point of the religious contribution of the plain person is his interest in self-discovery and family building.

The I in Me and the You in Thee

The simpler life of return to the natural has religious meaning because of its promise of opening up the "I" within each of us, for self-discovery and personal exploration. The advertising executive who chucked over his position and moved to a California beach readily admitted the (as usually understood) selfish element in the new naturalism. One wants to exchange the typical deferral of pleasure and fulfillment (which marks middle-class life) for joy and happiness right here and now. One seeks to make one person happy—himself. Extreme selfishness is overcome, however, when we consider the psychological truth that one can make others happy only when he is happy himself. The strengthening of self, the building of ego, is the surest way to build up the family, and the new adventurers in the simple life are very interested in the family. For the most part, the plain person is not interested in communes or group marriages, but is committed to the rehabilitation of the nuclear family. This emphasis upon the pair-bond and its children is another of the really conservative elements in the new naturalism. The modern pressures that have been splitting the family apart are rejected, and the pair-bond is put into a situation where the daily activity serves to upbuild the marriage.

Marriage Building?

Whether the move to a simpler (and physically harder) life will upbuild a marriage or tear it down depends, of course, upon who the two people are within that marriage bond. There are many marriages that would simply fall apart if the husband had to work physically from dawn to dark to raise the family's food, or if the wife had to walk a mile to a spring to get water and to wash clothes by hand in a creek. There are husbands who are too psychically fatigued by the pressures of modern society to cut their lawns, much less plow forty acres. There are middle-class housewives who are too psychically demoralized and dissipated by their psychotic separation from the real world to vacuum their houses without suffering exhaustion. How did the great-great-grandparents of these white families ever cross the North American continent on foot and horseback? Where was the electricity and the air-conditioning then? Are we a different species? In all events, there are few middle-class families that could or would stay together in a return to the life of the pioneer. The plain life will upbuild a marriage only if that marriage is between two healthy, hard-working, realistic persons who are oriented toward their bodies and the testing (not the coddling) of them. Most of our marriages and the people in them, including the many neurasthenic, spoiled children, would perish if they were forced to return to a pioneer style of life.

Yet, there are thousands of marriages and of couples who live together, who would and could adopt a new naturalism. These are worldly, body-oriented people, with a high degree of disgust at the way our society has destroyed the health and beauty of man and nature. All too often, the pioneer, in the eighteenth century and in the twentieth century, takes on the harsh challenge of the frontier because of his rejection of and by the society that produced him. The pioneer, then and now, was and is often a rebel. Often, too, the pioneer is a disappointed social activist—we forsake the facts when we forget that Siberia and rural Maine are frontiers. Rejected in Antioch and Jerusalem, Paul flees across the world to Asia Minor and Greece. There is personal disappointment and societal rejection in the history of most pioneers, and the new pioneers of the 1970's are not exceptions to the rule. Through the years of social upheaval and changing life-styles that I have studied North American culture, I have been forced to observe that the single most fulfilling and strengthening factor in a marriage is the devotion of both parties to a radical cause. This cause may be religious, sexual, artistic or political. The content is indifferent so long as it is radically different from the bland taste of the mainline culture, thus pushing man and woman (and children) together since it pulls them apart from the soporific verbiage and values of society. Those who "talk about the Lord" or talk revolution find that they usually are talking to one another, and that is the basis of marriage. The new naturalism is a radically new outlook and set of values, and thus does upbuild a pair-bond which has two dedicated people in it. The demands for physical and marital energy put on one by the effort to live a simpler life soon will show whether such dedication is real or imagined.

The churches are busy pulling in their horns of former social interest all around us. Churchmen are interested in rebuilding their depleted congregations and raising money. Meanwhile, while pastors are sticking close to their own parishes and wearing beads to youth meetings, the number of divorces among their suburban members are rising, drunkenness is increasing, and the inner cities continue to rot toward some new conflagration in the future. The plain people have a lot to teach the churches. Perhaps their absent bodies might get the message across.

CHAPTER 5
ART AND THE
NEW PLAINNESS

In the 1930's and 1940's, there was clearly an image of striking beauty and handsomeness communicated by the films and plays of the period. The plain, the ugly, the grotesque was relegated to horror films or to the comic. There was plenty of the nonbeautiful to be sure, but its popularity turned precisely upon its ridiculousness. Charlie Chaplin, W. C. Fields, the Marx Brothers, Laurel and Hardy, the Three Stooges, and the Bowery Boys showed us citizens who were anything but examples of beauty, hard work, courage, and intelligence. Millions laughed at them and with them, but the heroes and heroines of the time were the muscular and the smooth-featured, while the comics were shown as part of the warm-up to the main feature. When we look about us in the 1970's, the amazing thing is that of the great actors of the 1930's and 1940's, only the rough-featured Humphrey Bogart, surely the plainest featured movie star of all time, is as widely known to the youthful cinema public as the far-out comedy stars like Charlie Chaplin and W. C. Fields.

An old Pennsylvania Dutch proverb says: "Kissin' don't last, cookin' do." We may update that by saying that beauty doesn't last, but the plain-featured, even in Hollywood's movies, seem to last and last; speaking, decades later, to audiences that are made up of what are, after all, plain people, too.

We are all familiar with the fact that Hollywood was struck a heavy blow by the development of television. The number of paid admissions to movies dropped drastically after the introduction of the home television set on a mass basis. The great spectacles with their lavish scenery and highly paid stars had to shrink. Only a very few of the old superstars were enabled to continue. Later, as the studios were able to get in on the production of films for television the situation tended to work itself out, but at first, it seemed that the era of the motion picture was over. Even now, however, the unemployment rate in motion picture industrial unions runs up to 80 percent.

Throughout this period of strain, and continuing up to today, the zany cartoon continues in popularity. The movies did not die, they seemed to go underground. Every college campus witnessed the rise of the film festival that often zeroed in on Humphrey Bogart, Charlie Chaplin, or W. C. Fields. I have yet to hear of a John Wayne festival, or a Rita Hayworth, a Carole Lombard, a Clark Gable, or a Betty Grable festival. However, the attraction to plainness surfaced when a student recently told me that she liked John Wayne now because he was old, gray, and fat in *True Grit*. She said she liked bald and gray men. In looking over the films booked into college dormitories for weekly showings or by conference committees for yearly festivals, we find Lon Chaney, Boris Karloff, Bogart, Chaplin, and Fields. The two major cinema heroes of the present student generation are not the hip young stars of the surfing and motorcycle movies, but Charlie Chaplin who attacked fascism and the meaninglessness of industrial society, and W. C. Fields whose great contribution was to satirize the middle-class mores of industriousness, cleanliness, sobriety, good manners, and "seriousness." Both Chaplin and Fields were famous for just walking away. Hundreds of people today are just walking away down the road, too.

If we were to ask ourselves why Chaplin and Fields, who are so obviously dated, can still speak to this generation, we would have to begin answering our question by noting the similarities between these stars and the image of the countercultural person today. Both Chaplin and Fields are snipers who take devastating potshots at the overlord culture. They are effective in showing the feet of clay under our wealthy free-enterprise system. They subtly and not so subtly show the hypocrisy involved in the overlord standards of morality. They bring us mirth because they free us from the spell of propaganda that catches us when our critical faculty goes to sleep. Fields and Chaplin both remind us that the self-destructiveness of conformity and resistance to change was not removed from the world by the overthrow of the great dictator, Adolf Hitler. In particular, Chaplin's movie *Modern Times* seems very up-to-date, with its indictment of the dehumanization of the assembly line and of the refusal of businessmen to take seriously the humanity of those who are not contributing cogs in the great machine of commerce. Chaplin is a knight tilting against the monstrous windmill of the industrial state, or if you will, a Weatherman destroying the computer of a large university.

Fields is the eternal subversive. Walking through the small towns that are the scenes of his movies, Fields rejects the public flow of consciousness for an escape into the world of his own. That is the point of his always being drunk. He doesn't mind how high the cost of living goes or if war comes and blows the country sky high, he is already higher than the bomb. He lives in his own world, a world that has rejected the repressions that Freud tells us are the necessary sacrifices we make to have a civilization.

When we leave the theater, after laughing with W. C. Fields and Chaplin at our highly developed society, most of us are glad to drive to our comfortable rooms in our comfortable cars. We even stuff our mouths with the products of this exploitative civilization while the actor vents the outrage he and we feel over the estranging qualities of our culture. We do not, usually, go berserk and strip off our clothes, logically (from a rejection of civilization viewpoint) destroying all cultural artifacts, including the movie projector and screen. Rather, we rise to a peak of joy in howling at the contradictions and absurdities of a culture we love as well as hate. Our laughter is reformatory, peacefully revolutionary. Our weapon is satire and laughter, with an aim at helping and healing rather than destroying.

W. C. Fields' comedies are absolute scandals against the values of the mainline culture. He is surly, cynical, hates children, lies, stays drunk, and plays around with other women. He casts aspersions on everything the overlord culture holds sacred. And we love him for it. Fields lives by luck, not by law. He is as much a symbol of the outlaw, of the outsider, as the mobster or the Western bandit. Fields is everyman asserting his freedom and his will to pleasure and self-determination against the repressions that make up the foundations of society as we know it. He is a rebel with a cigar and a nasty mouth instead of a grenade and a machine gun. Our children celebrate his saving cynicism by imitating "W. C. Fritos" before the television every night. Every time I see one of my children with a "W. C. Fritos" eraser on his pencil, I know that somehow they are healthy because they have smelled the rat in our society, too.

Charlie's Crusade

Chaplin is also a gentle revolutionary. His silly costume and shiny hat, his cane and painted face are his uniform in the war against conformity and the stifling of human feelings and desires. Chaplin stands for the human sentiment, the urge to touch, to kiss, to laugh, that destroys the discipline and regimentation that both Karl Marx and Henry Ford believed were necessary for industrial production. Chaplin is the grandfather not only of a great tradition in movies and a million posters, but also of the youthful zanies (the Yippies) who declared that the revolution could be promoted by making love in the streets. His destruction of the production line in the film *Modern Times* is the forerunner of the monkey warfare of today that punches extra holes in computer cards or leaves parts off cars on the assembly lines. Chaplin was a nonconformist in life as well as on screen and years before the emergence of the counterculture lived his own free lifestyle. He paid the price of nonconformity, and only in extreme old age, received the honors from Hollywood he had earned long before World War II. Whatever his flaws, and Chaplin had them as all men do, his movies stand for the powers of life over against the powers of death. For that reason, Chaplin is a giant symbol of and influence on the art of our time.

Bogie

Humphrey Bogart was always an improbable movie "hero." An outsider with every atom of his being, Bogart rose to fame as the man who somehow didn't fit in any social situation in which he was found. Always the disappointed idealist, the cynic who has lost his faith, he manages, in the end, to attain a glimpse of the human vision again. His movement from unbelief to belief, from noninvolvement to involvement laid the basic groundwork for such recent films as *Blow-Up* and *Bonnie and Clyde*. The movement toward commitment, from selfishnesss and rejection, so graphically presented in Bogart's films makes a powerful appeal to the searching youth of today.

Bogart is always on the outs with the system, no matter what that system may be. He is the criminal, the bank robber, in the Depression years of the United States. He is the Resistance sympathizer in Vichy-controlled North Africa. He is the bystander, neither identifying with the victims nor the criminals in *Key Largo*. Bogart's wall of indifference, his withdrawal from pain, is clearly portrayed. The whole dramatic action of his movies is his warming up to human relationships and his final commitment of himself to others. *Casablanca* is Bogart's classic statement of this theme—a rejection of the system but an eventual commitment to persons—the basic value of the counterculture today. Yet this movement from depersonalization to personhood is not always posssible in the corruption of the world. Bogart also represents the rebel who fights until he dies; the eternal nay-sayer that finds freedom in death. The ending of *High Sierra,* with its death by long distance, carried by the crack of the telescopic rifle, is brutal and moving at the same time. As the bank robber crumples under the high-powered bullet and the little dog whines, we are reminded of the grasping hand of the fatally struck soldier at the end of *All Quiet on the Western Front,* and of the wounded ex-college professor, fighting fascism to the death, at the end of *For Whom the Bell Tolls.* In this world, in cinema and in life, there is freedom for some, it seems, only in fighting until they fall. In each of these films, however, there is a note of humanistic optimism. Bogart's robber has learned to love the girl and the little dog. The soldier has made his own separate peace and is reaching for a butterfly as he dies. The American volunteer is giving his life for the Spanish girl he loves, as well as for a just political cause. People, other people, have claims upon us that redeem us and make us whole and happy, even at the point of death, these films declare. Bogart and the Hemingway and Remarque films give us the value system of the counterculture, the ethic of the person who has moved beyond beauty and luxury.

Humphrey Bogart, almost alone of the Hollywood stars, shows us a pattern of alienation from modern society that gradually moves (in most of his movies) toward reentry into the human race. Bogart is the rejector of society and its systems, first for his own selfish withdrawal from society, then for the sake of the little people he has come to love. The difference between Bogart and Chaplin lies in one point only—that Chaplin begins each film with a love for the small person as well as with a hatred of the system, while Bogart has to suffer toward the growth of personality that allows him—sometimes—to love.

The counterculture, both of the beat and the hippie generations, have their roots in films such as these, as well as in the novels and plays of the 1930's and 1940's. The plain person, too, identifies with the eternal subversives, pleading for the personhood lost in the cruelties of a mass society.

Films and the Shaping of Our Consciousness

If you find it strange to have the countercultural consciousness explicated in terms of films that are decades old, stop and ask yourself, what media—or even what experiences—have gone into the shaping of our minds in our lifetime? If you analyze well, you will find that film, in the cinema, the classroom and on television has been the overarching shaper of our ideals and ideas. Just as the Athenians of old best saw the foundations of their religion and culture in the plays presented annually in their outdoor civic theaters, we North Americans come to terms with our foundational beliefs, hopes, and fears in the movies. You bet the counterculture has its inception in films, and by films it is extended! The whole world is watching when ideals are presented on the screen and that mass exposure, with its silent invitation to participate in those ideals, creates a culture. The Russians were not wrong to attempt to use the cinema to spread Communist ideals, nor was Hitler's Nazism wrong in its emphasis on the usefulness of the film.

The foundational role of the cinema in the formation of the minds of the generations from sixty down to six can be illustrated in many ways. I often hear people remark that certain things they have experienced themselves do not seem "real" until they see them on television or in the movies. The most outrageous—and yet true—example I can think of was the turning out of Marines on relief from the lines in Korea to watch John Wayne's Marine combat films during their respites from combat. These men ate up the World War II movies and expressed the desire to have a warm war like that. One wonders if policemen watch the cops and robbers programs regularly? Reality, for our era, is more than what one can taste and feel, it is what we see and hear—on the screen as well as in "life."

Pornography, Violence, and the Continuing Subversion of the Overlord Culture

The subversion of the mainline culture by films today seems to be the province of the films of ultraviolence, such as *Bonnie and Clyde* and the movies of ultrasex that flood our X-rated theaters.

The essence of the youth culture, overall, is rock music. The essence of the plain person thrust of the counterculture is getting free, socially, mentally, physically, and spiritually from the conformity of our technological, overlord culture. The essence of the middle-class culture, itself riddled with contradictions, seems more and more to be a fascination with violence and open sexuality. Films, television, novels, plays all show this interest. Moralists often attribute the increasing visibility of pornography and/or eroticism to the counterculture, but a closer examination reveals the essentially middle-class, older person origin and direction of heavily sexual matter. It isn't hard to test this assertion. Just attend one of the X-rated movie houses and check the people who attend. You won't find many younger people. You will find the middle-aged. The crude sex and four-letter words of these films stand in sharp contrast to the stress on a new plainness, a new asceticism that is growing out of the counterculture today.

"Skin flicks," as they are called, cannot be considered a part of the plain person culture, simply because of their artificiality and their obvious aim at unfree personality traits. Indeed, it is hard to understand why people who hold to the essential artificialities of social conventions would need to "escape" from daily subjection to those conventions by attending such films. My research, which includes teaching an experimental course on the effect of pornography on people at a state university, tends to bear out the contention that most younger people find X-rated films boring.

Pornography's rise to prominence in the last decade seems less an aspect of the counterculture and more of a counterrevolutionary thrust of the overlord, economically exploitative culture to me. It is, above all else, a way to make lots of money out of people's hang-ups and weaknesses. Tickets to such shows are $3-$5. The essentially impersonal, voyeur orientation of sex films is neither a simple approach, a natural attitude, or a warmly human outlook on sex. It is not the depiction of sexual activity that is misguided, but the kind of attitude toward sexual behavior and the impersonal, selfish way sexuality is handled that is completely wrongheaded. The appeal is to the unthinking and the unfeeling elements in immature personalities. The explicitly sexually oriented film—and stage play, book, and "dirty story"—is directed toward the elements of selfishness and alienation in everyone of us. The claim sex films and pornography makes upon us is upon the voyeur in us, that is, the portion of our personalities that is less than fully human. The plain person must reject this material, because he knows that the voyeur, the looker, is one who is unable to engage himself with the world and others in that world. The looker is forever separated from others by his inability to feel other persons as real and as important as himself. The plain person rejects this way of being in the world both on moral-religious grounds as well as on the basis that full involvement with a living human being is more satisfying in sex and in everything else than the godlike looking at others of the voyeur.

A better approach to the art of the new plainness would be through the humorous deconditioning of the American mind from its fixation on violence. Such movies as *M*A*S*H*, and the subsequent television serial of the same name, show the ridiculous nature of military operations. The famous book *Catch-22*, by Joseph Heller and the movie later made from it, explore the same theme, the foolishness of violence.

One of the major interests of the plain person, simplicity movement is the achieving of the deconditioning of the mind from the ordinary acceptance of inhuman values by people who have been spiritually calloused by the ceaseless grind of violence, overconsumption and sex in films, television and mass advertising. We have been reared in an atmosphere, a consciousness that presents mayhem, death, destruction, and hate, as well as selfishness, self-seeking, and the lust for sensual pleasure as the essentials for life. Little children are bombarded by cartoons that are violence-ridden, like the zany, but distressing, episodes of *Roadrunner*. The Saturday (and Sunday) morning cartoon features are full of violent acts, weapons, and struggle. The movies we see in theaters and on TV are sagas of murder, arson, beatings, and violent actions in words and deeds. We are so conditioned to this state of affairs that we think nothing of the gore and brutality that forms the backbone of our "entertainment." Ironically, parents and preachers become disturbed over the presentation of human sexuality but not over dehumanizing brutality. Yet, to this date, we have no social scientific proof that viewing sexual material harms young people but we do have studies that show that viewing violence inclines children toward violent acts themselves. The situation is analogous to that of alcohol and marijuana. We have plenty of evidence as to the destructiveness of alcohol and none as to the harmful effects of marijuana. We refuse to consider the legalization of the unholy "weed," however, while allowing alcohol to dominate the social life of the country. A visitor from Mars would find it difficult to understand our society as a rational one.

The exploitative mainline culture also becomes upset over the movies, books, and speeches of countercultural types that draw aside the veil of our accustomed acceptance of violence in films to reveal its real demonry. The stomach-turning wounds and killings presented in the films *Catch-22*, *M*A*S*H*, *Bonnie and Clyde,* and other recent films are criticized. Why? Because they are too realistic—it is "better" to think that the cowboy shoots the Indian who cleanly falls off his horse far off in the background of the movie. Like capital punishment, the film also hides the reality of death. We want a clean, private execution in the prison's electric chair room, not a public display of hanging. But films like *Bonnie and Clyde* force the killing and wounding of others out of the closet into the full light of day—the murder of the bank employee isn't done at a distance, but up close, in the midst of the silliness of the inept robbers' getaway. We have to stomach, if we can, what it means to take another person's life. That honesty ought to be the rule in films and TV—no killing or mayhem unless it is honestly and sickeningly made realistic—then there would be less of it shown.

The latest wave of art in the counterculture is humor—the critical humor of the person who feels himself consciously outside of the major culture. "The Fire-Sign Theater," a group of long-standing, continues to parody the ways of the corporate, government-controlled world. The raucous records of Cheech and Chung satirize everything from the Vatican to politics.

With the way-out comedy routines of the Fire-Sign Theater and Cheech and Chung, we come close to the center of the counterculture, the subworlds of drugs and the occult. Most of the comedy of the Fire-Sign Theater, which is chiefly "dug" by "heads" or dope users, concerns itself with the "stoned" or drug experience. The famous line from one of their records, about a bus ride, is "We're all bozos on this bus." A bozo is a head—a freak in the absolute sense. Cheech and Chung also allude heavily to the dope experience although they also criticize daily life. Listening to these records (and they are quite popular with the young of high school and college age, because of their irreverent comments on society), we feel ourselves pushed toward the outer limits of reason—toward the edge. Beyond the edge, there is the occult.

The Occult and Art

The materials we usually consider part of the occult have historically been part of art. The mandala, demons, angels, Satan, and magic are all part of painting, drawing, sculpture, poetry, and drama. The Middle Ages, the Renaissance, and the Victorian era all demonstrated high occultic interest in the arts. For the past decade popular art and culture has returned to images drawn from mythology, religion, and especially the occult.

For the occultist, and there are many among us, in and out of the counterculture, life is a vast game—a masque in which good and evil play out their parts on the pages of history. The man of the occult, in religion as in art, is that man who has studied to discern the active powers of good and evil at work in the world. He has subordinated his whole life to his knowledge of good and evil, and spends his time watching for signs of these powers' influence in his own life and in affairs around him. For him, every moment in life is a situation in which he must fend off the forces of evil and summon up the powers of good. He continually looks for a sign, any sign, as to how the cosmic forces are swinging in their pre-ordained ways. His whole being is devoted to the enormous possibilities of success or disaster that may come on the morrow by the turning of the wheel of fortune. He must live on tip-toe, and on guard, for there is no loyal heavenly Father for him and he possesses no trust in God—his life depends upon the signature of the stars in his hand and upon the swinging pendulum of fate.

The life-style of the plain person is not necessarily bound up with the occult, any more than it is with drugs. I hope to point out that the occult may be a part of the plain person's life-style without being taken too seriously. I trust that I have shown that drugs are antithetical to the very foundational beliefs of the plain person's culture.

Don Juan's Knowledge

One thing makes magic a continual source of interest and attraction to us; in magic, in the never-never land of once-upon-a-time, the ugly duckling can become a swan. In the case of Carlos Castaneda, the modern-day sorcerer's apprentice, we have a three-volume story of how just such an ugly duckling became an occultic swan—returning to nature at the same time. Just here we must suggest that perhaps we need to keep nature, and the way of listening to nature, distinct from magic. After all, Don Juan never tells Carlos that he is doing magic, only that he is acting as a man of knowledge. Perhaps that knowledge is a knowledge of nature's way.

In Carlos Castaneda, the way of the occult and the way of the more simple life (as well as the way of the dope user, at a certain level) tend to fuse into each other. Don Juan has become the cult hero of many thousands among the intellectuals and the nonintellectuals today, although his very existence is in doubt.[1] Carlos Castaneda does exist, and in him the virtues of the simple life, self-effacement, the desire for privacy and the search for self-knowledge, are very clear. Castaneda, whether from his own accumulated wisdom or from the teachings of Don Juan, teaches us that "not what you do, but what you don't do is most important to you." This is a good example of the gospel of addition by subtraction. The question we must face is, is this wisdom obtainable only through the occult, or is it not really available in our Christian faith and in eyes open to nature?

The new *Weltanschauung* or world outlook Castaneda calls "seeing" or "stopping the world." "Seeing" is more than looking or analyzing. Indeed, it is an absence of analyzing, a movement away from looking at things in our everyday way. It is a viewing of the world nonjudgmentally, without preconceptions. Castaneda says that then the world becomes a place of mystery, beauty and, altogether, a different, a separate reality.

I found Castaneda's books wholly believable as a Western-educated man whose mind was stretched to the breaking point by his submergence in a totally foreign way of looking at the world. Whatever the truth about the existence of Don Juan as a person, Castaneda gives us a world of internal consistency in his three books—a truly novelistic world in which the character that is developed is his own. Much of the critique of Western civilization made explicitly by Don Juan in these books and implicitly given by Castaneda's conversion to Don Juan's outlook, is on target and correct. Yet the beauty and attractiveness of Castaneda's move from our common sense naive realism to a more open, mystery-filled way of life is not really dependent upon the occult or magic. Don Juan's way to "knowledge" is rather a way of purgation, a way of truly "stopping the world" which our culture has made, so that we might bathe in the mystery and beauty of nature and of life itself again. Don Juan's message is that of C. G. Jung—all life is synchronicity—a unity orchestrated out of many seemingly separate parts.

I am also reminded of Dietrich Bonhoeffer's description of Jesus Christ and his work in *Ethics* when I think of Don Juan. Bonhoeffer stresses the unseparated unity of Jesus with God that issued in a way of simplicity in his life.[2] Bonhoeffer tries to teach us that the Christian life is to be noncalculating, unhurried, uncritical, and simple.

It is this simplicity that draws the plain person. That teaching of "letting go," of "not doing," is what is attractive in Carlos Castaneda for the counterculture, and for all of us, today.

One of the continuing influences upon the whole counter-cultural movement, and especially of significance for the plain person, is the heritage of the American Indian. T. C. McLuhan, a Canadian writer, has done a fine job of collecting old photographs of some of the Indian leaders and people of the later nineteenth century, along with a selection of their sayings.[3] Again and again, the Indian gives us the expression of a natural piety that is a simple sense of identification with nature. Walking Buffalo, a Stoney Indian of Canada, is reported to have said to the Whites:

We were lawless people, but we were on pretty good terms with the Great Spirit, Creator and Ruler of all. You whites assumed we were savages. You didn't understand our prayers. You didn't try to understand. . . . We saw the Great Spirit's work in almost everything: Sun, moon, trees, wind and mountains. Sometimes we approached him through these things.[4]

Such simplicity, such involvement in another reality, is profoundly moving and attractive to the plain person today. We are convinced that the society that has put shoes on our feet has also cut us off from the world itself. Like the Man of La Mancha we are alienated from the "reality" around us. We tilt at the windmills that we vaguely feel are something more than windmills, knowing in our bones that the only sane people today are those called "crazy."

The Man of La Mancha, the utopian visionary of the impossible dream, is a good symbol of the modern counter-culture. The social reform, the breakthrough to a new level of consciousness on the part of the bearers of the new mentality does amount to a utopian, messianic movement. The issue is not just to change society, but to allow man to change. It is a thorough-going psychic revolution that the plain person holds in view.

The sensitivity of plainness is best seen in handicrafts and in the painting, drawing, and pottery of new mentality members. It can be seen, too, in the poetry and literary works stemming from this source. I recall one young boy in Minneapolis asking me why I was taking notes on what he was telling me when I was researching *The New Mentality* in 1967. When I told him I was planning a book on the new form of consciousness I had discerned in his generation, he expressed surprise that I would want to write about it. "Why not just enjoy it?" he asked.

The plain person outlook has a political edge, the ecology movement, but it is not primarily a political phenomenon. It is rather a return to the development of the person, the family, and the small group. The people who rise to a change in consciousness are those who expect a new world to come by changes in philosophy, not changes in power relations. Sometimes there is a temptation to simply reject the "progress" or "evolution" of our society, hoping to thus "get back" to the natural man.

The quest for a fuller, yet simpler life is distorted and often wrecked by too simple-minded a bent toward utopianism. This is a rather dogmatic statement, to be sure, yet one that can be illustrated from human history—as Paul Tillich does in his critique of utopianism[5]—as well as from our day-to-day experience in today's world.

One utopian ideal that has received much energy and attention of late has been the concept of "open marriage," put forth by Nena and George O'Neill.[6] Much of the O'Neills' analysis and recommendations is healthful and in the line of new consciousness, but their idea that an "open marriage" might involve open sexual intercourse with persons outside the marriage is utopian—at best.[7] A minister recently told me of the damage caused to the marriage of two of his best friends by too utopian an adoption of this possibility. His friends went on vacation with another couple with whom they had been discussing the book *Open Marriage*. Over the weekend they decided to put the sex-swapping into effect. The couples paired off with the spouse of the other couple for the night. One partner, a husband, found that he only talked with his female companion. He enjoyed the experience and reported it to his own wife the next morning. She was immediately crushed, for she had not only talked but engaged in sexual intercourse. The husband assured her that such activity was part of the "contract" they had made, but it did no good. She is still depressed about the experience, months later.

How much better if those couples had followed the less utopian but very freeing concept of synergy, explored in the same book, *Open Marriage*.[8] In synergy, or an enhanced combination of two people, each person brings himself or herself to enjoy giving the other partner pleasure. This is the same relationship that the parent has with the child, as when the mother enjoys seeing the child enjoy himself. The O'Neills suggest that in open marriage synergy can be enhanced so that what is good for one can be seen as better for both.[9]

Unredeemed Nature Is Brutality and Violence

(The Lesson of *Deliverance* and *A Man Called Horse*)

The old theologians spoke of "natural evil" as well as "human evil," meaning earthquakes, storms, and tidal waves. Natural evil covered all those untoward events that lawyers and insurance companies call "acts of God." In addition to this natural misfortune, there is the agony brought on man by man himself. No one who has lived in a more dependent state on nature than the city dweller could ever honestly believe that nature, in the raw, was kind. No one could deduce a good God from man's experiences with nature. Consider the Nicaraguan earthquake, the Japanese tidal waves, the explosion of the volcano at Krakatau. Unredeemed nature may well be beautiful, but it is crude, brutal, and often violent. Even the lonely forests of the tropics are full of snakes, insects, and disease and the men who live there in a more "natural" state than the urban people of America, are frequently murderous and also ignorant and sick. The "nature" to which one who has moved beyond beauty and luxury wishes to return—whether he knows it or not—is a redeemed, not an unredeemed nature.

Two recent films bring home the brutality and coarseness of man in the more "natural" state quite well. One is *Deliverance,* by poet James Dickey of the University of South Carolina, about four white men who seek to return to unspoiled nature and find death. The other film is *A Man Called Horse,* which is based on excellent ethnological studies, about the Sioux Indians of the nineteenth century. This film is full of as much brutality and violence, all based scientifically on primitive man's customs, as you would ever want to see. Unredeemed, or as theologians sometimes say, natural—man is no lover of peace and flowers. What the plain person really is looking for in the simple "natural" life is redeemed, pious, and "civilized" man. The myth of a lost paradise and a devolution toward greater sinfulness through urban, civilized development simply won't hold historical water. We will all be better off, in both the mainline and the counterculture, once we get that perfectly clear. A simple utopianism based on a false myth is of no help to the millions of people who thirst, long, and are dying inside for a new culture with a more human way of life.

What the new mentality, expressed now in the plain person's search for happiness beyond beauty and luxury, after all, is, in religious terms, is a new humanity, a redeemed mankind. That redemption, as Genesis correctly points out, will not come simply by building a tower of Babel taller than the John Hancock tower or the World Trade Mart. Such redemption comes only from God and must be experienced deep in the spiritual guts of those who are open to receive it. The need for such a redemption, and the nonbrutal, human communion it makes possible, explains why those communes based on religious principles (and/or disciplines) have the best chance of success in this era of social experimentation. The wide-openness of those new pioneers who are seeking to find themselves and to rebuild their family lives is the appropriate stance of those who are waiting for that redemption we all vaguely feel the need of—and some of us deeply thirst for.

CHAPTER 6
FEED YOUR HEAD—
A NATURAL PHILOSOPHY

The most open temptation any American faces is the lure of sentimentality. Most peculiarly, the observer of current problems must face, and conquer, this temptation in himself, for it is far to easy to contrast the "mess of today" with "the good old days." That this temptation is universal is proven by the existence of reaction everywhere at every time (note the Nazis' in the 1920's and 1930's) underscored by the often quoted observations of Confucius and Socrates about the degeneracy of their days. For the American, the temptation usually lies in an unrealistic view of the past, and especially of the native American, the Indian. Sentiment has painted the Indian in colors of every hue—from a blood-thirsty murderer to a Stoic Roman philosopher living peacefully with nature. In using the Indian as an example we need to guard ourselves against both extremes, yet, once the balance is struck, we do find much to admire and to emulate in the life-styles of the original Americans.

Living with, Not Ripping Off the Land

The Indians, by and large, saw themselves as "men," as the creatures called mankind that made up a peculiar place in the natural order of things. The Indians never felt that they should—or could—change the face of the earth that supported them. They might cut a tree, even burn off an area, but nothing on a grand scale. Their farming was limited and adapted to the grains and vegetables native to their area. Animals were regularly hunted, but none were killed without a purpose—for food. For decades the Plains Indians lived off the vast, shifting herds of bison or American buffalo without depleting their numbers. Then, in the space of a decade, the white hunters almost destroyed the buffalo—wasting the carcass for the sake of the hide.

It is this white European urge to fully exploit that marks the difference between the American settler and the native American Indian. Where the Indian walked, the forest soon closed over his footprints, where the white man's boots trod, the forest and the animals died.

The Indians, in general, felt that nature was sacred; for the most part, the Whites did not share this sentiment. The earth and its resources lay before the settler as the source of riches—something to be used and changed, in distinction from the Indian philosophy of living in harmony with nature. Many famous quotations from Indians have survived that tell of their astonishment at the "inhuman" attitude of the Whites toward the world and its creatures. In a large way, the new pioneers are aiming at more of an Indian style of life than at an early settler style of life. This is a profound difference, which makes the plain person of today something of a living act of contrition for the way his ancestors misused the land.

Chief Luther Standing Bear made this incisive insight in his autobiography, published as recently as 1933:

The white man does not understand the Indian for the reason that he does not understand America. He is too far removed from its formative processes. The roots of the tree of his life have not yet grasped the rock and soil. The white man is still troubled with primitive fears. . . . The man from Europe is still a foreigner and an alien. And he still hates the man who questioned his path across the continent. But in the Indian the spirit of the land is still vested; it will be until other men are able to divine and meet its rhythm. Men must be born and reborn to belong. Their bodies must be formed of the dust of their forefathers' bones.[1]

Standing Bear may be still right about most of us, but among some Whites the process of rebirth may now be going on. Like the Indian and the Amish, there are arising men and women open to the soil and to new styles of living in skuzzy clothes, with less than the "American average man." Perhaps in these new, natural and plain people, Standing Bear would see hope for America. On both the territory of communes, like the Brotherhood of the Spirit in Massachusetts and the Lama Foundation in New Mexico, as well as on individual farms, people are searching for themselves, and for America.

Sue and Eliot Coleman have shifted from the life of college teaching and suburban living to rising at 5:45 A.M. to send Eliot out to the fields for two hours before breakfast while Sue puts a fire together in an old wood stove, grinds wheat into flour by hand and bakes Chappaties, a tortilla-like bread. Hauling their water from a spring, they wash in a small tub in the cabin. The Colemans are close to the soil and love it.

Gordon and Judy Harding left Louisville, Kentucky, where Gordon was picture editor of *The Louisville Courier-Journal*. At the top of his profession, Gordon found not pleasure but a constant tension and pressure. The frantic upward mobility of the middle-class suburb they lived in drove them to seek something better. Vacationing in Vermont, the Hardings found what they wanted—a simpler life, without social competition. Gordon bought land, built a garage where he now repairs Volkswagens, then built a two-story home on a mountainside with his own hands. The Hardings have found a "one-to-one" relationship with life, working with their hands, living close to nature, knowing people in depth. Free of pollution and pressure, they now seek to plumb the depths of what they can do themselves and of what they can experience in friendship with others.[2]

Bill and Ann Muller of Bucks County, Pennsylvania

have struck deep into the realm of imagination to find a happy life. The Mullers make wooden toys in a small shop in Dublin, Pennsylvania.[3] Their real joy is the pleasure children get out of their toys—which are safe and not too detailed, leaving room for childhood imagination. Here is an example of people finding a new, simpler life in a small town rather than on a farm. The Mullers are finding happiness by the stimulation of their own imagination and that of others. They feel that our society has spoiled childhood by the sophistication and mass availability of toys. "We love toys," Muller has said, "but most kids have too many. You know, we always had more fun playing with a bunch of cardboard cartons. A carton can be anything you want it to be. You just used your imagination. And that's what we do with our toys. Keep them simple, and give the kids a chance to imagine."[4]

Muller interrupts his work any time visitors arrive at the shop. It may be a busload of school children or retarded children or a nursery school. When they arrive Muller stops and plays. The children are encouraged to draw their own designs on wood, which Muller then cuts out for them.

Until 1968 Bill Muller was a $65,000-a-year owner and operator of a Baltimore trucking business. When the riots of that year wiped out his terminal he sold out and moved to Vermont with the aim of working with his great love—wood. Subsequently he combined this with his other loves—kids and toys—and launched a new career. The toys are made solely of wood with no screws, nails, or tacked-on parts. From a circus train and a logging truck to Crocky the Crocodile, Willie the Whale, and Myrtle the Turtle, the more than three dozen Muller designs are strong and imaginative. Kids "test" them almost daily in the shop and only those that seem to mean something to kids get reproduced. Being craftsmen and pleasing children has become the Mullers' business and their freedom.

Dorothy Kalins, traveling about the country gathering material for her book *Cutting Loose*,[5] found dozens of people who had left well-paying jobs, comfortable homes, and well-to-do life-styles to begin a simpler, more hardy way of life. She found that people generally move away from lawns back to the land where they can raise something more significant than their neighborhood prestige. People go to places they may have visited in childhood, or seen on a great vacation trip, to trees, the sea or a lake, to places without traffic jams, smog, crowds, and social pressures.

We probably all know people, by now, who have made choices similar to this—the stepping back from the normal career ladder, the move to a quieter pace, the more social and personal setting. In our parents' day men nearing fifty used to speak of buying a little "chicken farm" and settling down. Today there are a multitude of men and women in their twenties who see that goal as the only one that makes sense. Maybe we are growing up as a people, getting reborn. Standing Bear should be around today to tell us his impression.

Do We Really Know Which Way Is Up?

A society which rather firmly believes that it can borrow its way to prosperity and live the good life on the installment plan ought have no especial difficulties understanding the gospel of addition by subtraction. Indeed, both ideas sound outrageous on our first hearing them. Yet the idea that less may be more, the cultivation of a discipline of plainness and naturalness, has a long and sound historical background.

The Old Testament prophets were vehement in their denunciation of luxury and the lust for riches. Amos, Hosea, and Jeremiah all lashed out at the desire for wealth and rich living that marked the upper classes of their time. The prophets, like the author of the book of Judges, knew that Israel lost its faithfulness to Yahweh when soft living, and the love of it, spread throughout the land. Like our modern-day prophets, Amos and his fellow spokesmen for God knew that rich living on the part of the upper classes meant injustice, oppression, and grinding poverty for the lower classes. To learn to live with less, to share with one's fellowmen, to depend more on God, these traits would have spared Israel and Judah from the destruction that fell upon them. What is most striking in the twentieth century, to any observer, is that these biblical insights are the property of the most secular of men. Thousands, without formal religious affiliation, believe what the prophets preached, perhaps more than the clergy do.

Jesus Christ stood most clearly in the line of the prophets when he taught absolute dependence upon God, not on nature, but on the God who redeems nature. Jesus urged men to remember the birds of the air, which God cares for, and the flowers of the fields, which God dresses more richly than kings and queens. He taught us to "take no thought for tomorrow," to give up our outer cloak as well as our inner coat, to travel without sandals or wallet. The Messiah was a plain man and pointed to a plain and faithful way of life in his "ethics of the Kingdom." He who had no place of his own to lay his head lived happily and simply with the common people of the land.

Jesus, in many ways was more like the Man of La Mancha—fighting invisible forces and powers, or like Charlie Chaplin, wandering through the world doing good to little people—than he is like modern preachers. No president or governor ever asked Jesus to preach in their first-century "White Houses." The only time Jesus appeared in such places, he was under condemnation and made the object of cruel sport. The plainness of Jesus' life stands in the starkest contrast not only to the great figures of statecraft and war, but in contrast to popes, bishops, rabbis, and Protestant ministers of the past and of today. Despite the gold and silver crosses, the stained glass windows and fabulous churches of Christendom, the gospel record is clear. Jesus stands apart from all we think of as religious, not only for his spiritual and ethical elevation over all other men but for his simplicity, his plainness. Perhaps this is why even the most rabid opponents of religion have generally excluded Jesus from their critiques.

Paul was another plain man whose teachings might be taken as classic statements of the plain philosophy. Paul was a tent-making minister, who lived a simple life and supported himself with his own hands. He had simple tastes and once declared that he had learned to be content in whatever state he found himself. He, however, had no illusions about the world, for he knew that the world was bound under sin. He looked for the evidences of a redeemed humanity in his converts, stressing the need to care for one's own family and counseling a simple life of nonpretense (Ephesians 4:1-32; 5:1-20; Galatians 5:13-26; 1 Thessalonians 4:1-12; esp. 2 Thessalonians 3:6-13).

The early monks, too, sought to live plain, unadorned lives of quiet happiness in the service of God. They sought, in time, to serve their fellowmen also. During the so-called "Dark Ages" the monasteries became the repositories of civilization and as the ancient classical government of Rome broke down, and the barbarian tribes invaded what was previously civilized territory, the monasteries preserved the ancient arts and sciences.

Yet the monasteries also devolved and became more worldly and luxury-seeking in many cases. Indeed, it was against the un-monklike lives of many of the inhabitants of monasteries that much of the Protestant criticism was directed in the sixteenth century. Monasticism has been condemned so thoroughly by theologians and others that perhaps nothing we say would redeem it. In the modern world, even in the Roman Catholic Church, monasticism has lost its appeal in general. And yet, as we have seen throughout this book, the kinds of life-styles that characterized the monks have become more and more of interest to young people and older people today. Of course, we do not foresee communes in which the vows of poverty, chastity, and obedience would be taken, and yet something like a voluntary poverty and much voluntary obedience is involved in every communal experiment. If we are to cope with our rising obsession with sexuality, perhaps some voluntary chastity may even be required in the future.

The monastic ideal found its healthiest expression in Benedict of Nursia (who founded the monastery at Monte Cassino, Italy in A.D. 529), who dignified manual labor by teaching that monks should work as well as pray. In Francis of Assisi, monasticism was broken open altogether by love. The simple life of poverty and service to others has never been so remarkably lived by a human being—after Jesus—as it was by Francis. But apart from a few monks and idealistic missionaries, the life-style of Jesus, Paul, and Francis has not been seen in modern times. We think immediately of Dr. Tom Dooley's work in Indochina; Albert Schweitzer's work in Africa, and Mohandas Gandhi's great work in South Africa and India, and of a few other lives. Yet, many modern philosophy, theology, and religious studies have directed their attention to the recovery of the spirit underlying such a simpler style of life.

Dreaming Innocence or the Gentility of Civilization?

George Steiner, in a conversation reported in *Psychology Today*,[6] remarks upon the American reward for inarticulacy. In America, in contrast to the English tendency, there is a positive valuation of mumbling, halting speech. Americans view such Gary Cooper-like language as the mark of deep honesty, whereas the elevated, "slick," language of the articulate is looked upon with suspicion. Americans seem to distrust the glib, the intelligent, the highly verbal. They see a danger of being tricked or "conned" behind polished manners, dress, and speech. In fact, the archetypical figure of "Uncle Sam" developed from the stage presentation of a shrewd New England country trader during the nineteenth century. This says something about the way we inwardly view our government and business.

Somehow the story of the fast-talking snake in the Garden of Eden is lodged in our national consciousness. The tower of Babel story with its condemnation of the city and its sophistication also is taken as an indication that the simple, plain life of the countryside is more ethical and spiritual than urban living.

The ultimate philosophical foundation of such a high evaluation of the simple life, of the plain person, is the identification of the state of innocence with the state of ignorance. It is, on this view, learning and the desire for knowledge that has ravished the human race. Paul Tillich, giving mythological-type names to the story of Adam's fall, calls this the myth of dreaming innocence. Only in the twentieth century, spearheaded by such spiritual, yet highly intellectual minds as Carl Gustav Jung, Paul Tillich, Mircea Eliade, and Rollo May has the very dubious basis of this view been challenged. The stress placed on plainness, even ugliness or ungainliness, as the mark of innocence, with a high valuation of ignorance is now said to be quite wrong, morally. Rollo May uses the term pseudo innocence to refer to the denial of guilt feelings by the world.[7] Simply being ignorant of the fact that the slops we throw out of our top floor windows hit passersby on the street below does not make us innocent, but indifferent.

What, then, of the quest for the simple life today, of the desire to become a new pioneer? Insofar as these quests and desires are flights from the world, efforts to escape responsibility for other men, then such moves are examples of pseudo innocence. This moral stance is akin to that of fundamentalist-holiness groups that attach the quality of being or not being spiritual to the length of the hair, the wearing of jewelry or the use of certain words, foods, and drinks. Such efforts to be "holy" are not only simple but simple-minded, based as they are on the reasoning followed by those who would fraudulently wear a military uniform with medals they did not win. The analogy here is that looking courageous and brave does not make you courageous. Looking "holy" does not make one holy either. Looking "plain," dressing in old clothes, does not make one a truly redeemed person. There are many "hip-capitalists" who are as money-hungry as Daddy Warbucks.

If we ask the question, "What is the essential truth that lies beneath the rather shallow positive evaluation of simplicity in life-style?" we may get closer to the truth. The depth of reasonable truth that is embedded in the myth of dreaming innocence has to do with the possible transparency of human personality—its possible openness to other people and to the Divine.

Two Views of God and the World

It seems to me that there must be two contrasting ideas of the Divine that play a role in man's evaluation of the possibility of becoming open to God. One way is to see God as developing, indeed, as a process of more and more elaboration, now essentially incomplete; then, out there in the future, wholly manifest as the goal and aim of everything that is. This view would prize sophistication and would see the elaboration of culture, the development of more and more precise intellectuality, as evidences of becoming more spiritual. Such a vision of the Divine and its relationship to man is found in the works of Hegel, Spinoza, Whitehead, Teilhard de Chardin, as well as of Plato. This vision would see ignorance and simplicity as being worldly and unspiritual. Such an evaluation is included in the term pagan which originally referred to an unlettered countryman who still followed the old, pre-Christian religions. Augustine's use of the term "the City of God" as the description of the kingdom Jesus proclaimed is also based on the philosophical distinction between the civilized man and the materialistic barbarian.

But there is another vision of the Divine and of its relationship to man that is the exact opposite of the urbanized and intellectualized (Process) conception of development. Oftentimes this view, which I will call the simplistic, is mingled in with the developmental view in a contradictory way. This view is the one that lies at the base of the primal myth of Paradise. It sees Adam and Eve as being ontologically innocent, as being completely integrated with the Divine will until they began the process of learning. Learning turned them against God. It is as simple as that and as complex as that, for one has to ask what is the character of the Divine that it does not wish its creatures to share in knowledge? In all events Eve had the potentiality for knowledge in her curiosity and she swiftly actualized this by direct experience (Genesis 3:6-7). Once man had learned to discern good from evil, he was cursed. Cast out of Eden as rudely as an alarm clock awakens us from the dreaming innocence of an obsessive dream, man now finds it necessary to struggle through the waking day all the while tortured by the feeling that somehow he has lost a precious possession. There is no human being who has not felt this strange "nostalgia," regardless of its actual basis.

On the background of this mythic structure it is easy to see how the simple, the plain, even the ignorant can be evaluated as holy or close to the Divine. In some ways this view, which receives reemphasis in the Babel myth and a more or less philosophical development in the works of Jean-Jacques Rousseau, underlies the popularity of the simple life among many people in America today. Obviously both the elaborate or developmental view of the Divine and the simplistic view have deep consequences for Christian faith and life. Christian theology has produced a variety of anthropologies or visions of man, some more developmental, some more simplistic, and some a confused mixture of the two views.

William J. Lederer and Eugene Burdick, the novelists and critics of American foreign policy, made an "ugly" man the hero of their story of the mistakes made abroad in the foreign aid program. They pointed out that it takes a simple person who is completely human, living in good faith, to be accepted by simple people, anywhere and everywhere.

Thoreau's Contribution

Daniel J. Boorstin, the creative historian of America's experience, writing in *The Americans—The Democratic Experience*,[8] calls the nineteenth-century "developers" of the Western ranges, herds, mines, and Eastern railroads, trust and department stores, "the go-getters." Interestingly enough, he concludes his discussion of Rockefeller and Wild Bill Hickok with a discourse on organized crime. What we see as crime today may very well be the same manipulation of mankind and the environment that was called "progress" a century ago.

One nineteenth-century figure who was not a "go-getter," but the opponent of such attitudes, was Henry David Thoreau (1817-62). A writer, poet, and philosopher, Thoreau took the spiritual idealism of New England transcendentalism seriously and sought to live it fully. Henry David saw the still unspoiled countryside as the arena where the human spirit might unfold itself and fly. New England was not only the home of devout Congregationalists and Unitarians, it was also a seat of American capitalism—the fountain of "Yankee ingenuity." Thoreau rejected this go-getter mentality, asking "the life which men praise and regard as successful is but one kind. Why should we exaggerate any one kind at the expense of the other?"[9]

For Thoreau, the inner life, shaped by principle, was more important than the gaining of wealth and social honors. He desired an individual life-style for himself and declared that all others should have their opportunity for uniqueness, too. Henry not only wrote of the "different drummer," he was the different drummer in the American nineteenth-century parade. Out of Thoreau's imagination has come not only the rich New England literary tradition of unique characters and contributions but also the drive toward conservation and regional planning.

For Thoreau, the wide open expanses of the North American continent were opportunities for spiritual deepening of the person, not resources for exploitation. Unfortunately for our situation, the go-getters "got" the continent while Thoreau got only Walden Pond. Perhaps today the balance is being redressed, since Thoreau is now capturing the imagination of hundreds of thousands, as his ideas have proven more life-giving than those of the tough-minded Yankees who succeeded chiefly in spoiling our heritage.

By the end of his life, Thoreau had learned that the future could not be secured by an escape into primitivism alone. Man needs society and relations with many kinds of people to develop fully. However, he continued to call for the openness of civilization to the wilderness. America needs the opportunity the country affords for men to find themselves and their own peculiar genius. Thoreau's life and writings have borne fruit, fruit that has matured greatly in our own time.

Reflections

If that man or woman is most blest who needs least, if we should seek to develop our souls before we seek wealth and honors, and if we would be happier and wiser if we became indifferent to outward circumstances, what would this mean for our present-day society?

Would we immediately become nonconsumers? Would the state of our economy and social system be changed?

Apparently, the experience of plain people so far would not bear out a positive answer to this question. The Amish, for example, are consumers, but of simple things like farm equipment and plain black hats. Rather, plain people become consumers of different things, not nonconsumers. Consider the thousands of items advertised and discussed in the *Whole Earth Catalogue*. Plain people may give up conspicuous consumption, but they remain consumers of an outdoor or rural type. A society that suddenly saw millions of its people adopt the plain philosophy would be skewed, but not changed completely.

A more basic question is, would people who adopted the plain philosophy become more transparent to the divine, more open to love, more clearly reflective of the image of God? This is, after all, the healthy inner genius of the plain person view, in the declarations of Thoreau, of the prophets and of Jesus Christ.

To what degree does our general *nostalgie de la boue*, our yearning for a simpler past, represent an opening of men and women to the Spirit, and to what degree does it represent a flight from the prophetic demands of justice in the midst of our society's trials? Can the plain person movement be understood as another form of hubris, another way of showing selfishness? Is the reaction of withdrawal to the country but an exaggeration of the same flight from the undesired neighbors of the city we saw in the growth of the suburbs? Everyone who feels the tug of the plain philosophy must examine his own conscience on this score. The search for the simple may not be basically selfish, but it certainly could be pursued in a selfish way.

The philosopher Socrates (fifth century B.C.) pursued the plain life as an alternative to the supersophistication of Athenian culture. He was a secular monk, a moralist reminding men of the need to care for the inner life as well as the outer man. Jesus taught an indifference to outer circumstance based on absolute dependence upon God, who would care for every need if one bent his attention on his coming kingdom and sought its righteousness first. Why do men and women in our time respond to calls to attend to the inner life and to flee from the vanity of the world in our day? Is it out of concern for the full development of the human spirit? Is it a search for a moral alternative to a demoralizing way of life? Does faith in God play a role in this search?

Of course, there are no simple answers to such far-reaching questions. There are thousands of people involved in the simplistic-wing of the counterculture. Such people are, generally, truly individualistic, so their motives vary a great deal. We can discern selfish motives in some. We are convinced of spiritual motives in many. There are a number of motives involved in the withdrawal from the traditional ideals of success and status achievement in American society. I would say that these motivations are not found among the majority of people in North America, but are increasingly becoming live options for a significant minority. The minority to which I refer is, up to now, generally white and middle class, and I would characterize them as the issue-oriented. This is the same reservoir of people who provided the recruits for the civil rights movement and the peace movement. Among these social minded and democratically oriented persons in both the United States and Canada, as well as in other developed countries, the movement of concern over the population explosion arose as well as the environmental action movement with its fight against pollution and the quest for women's liberation. Today, under the impress of a number of setbacks for the wholly good yet idealistic goals they set for themselves, we are witnessing the rise of the plain philosophy as a form of withdrawal from a society dominated by powerful interests that do not care what is done to the world and its people as long as their profit and control is maintained. The plain philosophy is thus a form of isolationism, and can be compared with the withdrawal from the world in order to work out a better form of life such as that practiced by John the Baptist, Jesus' disciples, and the monastic communities of Christian history. In such movements of withdrawal, there is always a heavy element of spirituality even when it is not fully recognized by the individual person. On balance the individual selfishness inherent in escapism has always been outweighed by the achievement of new life-styles that promise a more human and moral social order. We can only hope that the same result will come from the new pioneering of our day.

Becoming Transparent

The Amish took to their isolated rural settlements, first in Europe, then in America, in order to more fully open themselves to the influence of the Spirit. Always fighting against the self-pride that is the constant temptation of the religious person, the original "plain people" sought for even greater conformity to the image of Christ. How successful any or all these dissenters have been in their search is, finally, a matter of opinion, but it is clear that they have promoted a peaceful social setting for human life that evokes our admiration. Growing into a scriptural pattern may very well demand more than a positive response, it may also involve the negative response of removing oneself from the distractions of the world. The monks and nuns of the Catholic tradition thought so, as do the Amish, Hutterites, and traditional Mennonites. Apparently, many modern Americans have come to the same conclusions without much reference to Christian history or world-rejecting theology. The Colemans desire nothing more than to give up all the advantages and trappings of American society, so as to live simply in the Maine woods. Others who have recently "chucked it" express opinions that sound very "Amish"—that automobiles have broken down neighborhoods while polluting the air we breathe and that fixed prices in chain stores from coast to coast have dehumanized the economic process. Such people have spread the practice of the garage sale, with its emphasis upon "rapping" and haggling over prices (that are nonexploitive) in order to resocialize men through "alternative economics."[10] Both those who are becoming new pioneers and those who are just thinking about the possibility need to consider alternative ways of life.

Some Alternatives

Becoming freer means being willing to give up money and things. It particularly means willingness to give up jobs with large organizations that offer many fringe benefits, including health insurance, life insurance, and retirement benefits. It includes, for many people, acceptance of a life on a lower salary in order to find more time for one's family, a cleaner, more crime-free environment and the opportunity to develop one's inner life and creativity. To adopt this new form of mentality one must be aware of opportunities for life-enhancement and the satisfactions that are either costless or less costly than the average urban activity. One must also, since he must eat, develop a liking for, and a skill in, shopping for bargains and learn how to make do with home repairs and less than the best available. Bargain hunting, buying in bulk, shying away from luxuries and prepared foods, are part of the plain person's life-style. As one person told me, "You have to be smarter than the average person to live as a poor person in this country."

Since we cannot completely withdraw from the North American economy, no matter where we may move to on the continent, the plain person must begin his break toward a freer life by becoming a saver. No matter how much we cut our consumption (and there is a point below which we cannot go), living takes some funds. It is well, then, to save while we are able, in order to provide a safeguard for our experiments at a freer life. Many people could make the break on the savings they have now, if they had the courage. Perhaps Americans and Canadians ought to consider seriously working toward an earlier retirement than sixty-five. By exercising control over our wants, and thus our spending, we will cut down on the pollution of the country—and of our lives—and perhaps find it possible to retire at age fifty.

After all, what do we need? Old clothes can be purchased at secondhand stores and even gotten free at free stores. We need no more than one suit. We can buy old furniture and fix it up ourselves. One urban pioneer told me that they drove around their city the night before the sanitation department picked up bulk items of trash and were able to pick up, free, chairs, tables, and sofas. Most of the things we need to operate a home can be secured, at fractions of their original cost, at the garage sales held every week in every neighborhood in the country.

A remodeled old house (do-it-yourself) is a possibility in many places. Often one does more than get cheap housing in this way. He also helps to improve a neighborhood. You can learn to cut your own hair or wear it long. Growing a beard saves razor blades and all the toiletry items we spend so much money on. There is no need to buy books if you have a library card. The health department gives shots free. There are free clinics operated by churches and other groups. To those who are becoming indifferent to outward circumstances, the world opens up, suddenly becoming freer than they ever thought it could be.

But to really be "free," we must become so inwardly. You can't fake being a new pioneer—for winter does come, illnesses develop, stomachs can get empty. You have to believe in what you are doing. One of the prophets sneered at the people of his day for worshipping the God of Israel and Baal at the same time. He told them to stop "limping between two opinions." We have to make up our minds, too. Either the old standards of Hollywood beauty and success are dead for us or they are not. Either the plain and simple are attractive and comfortable to us or they are not. We need a full break, inwardly, with the majority opinions or we are setting ourselves up for trouble. It is our heads that must be "gotten together" before we get our stuff together to move to the simple life.

In the last analysis, the plain philosophy is a call for repentance and conversion so that we might form a sacramental style of life. The young people who are moving in this direction need the help of the church and its theologians as much as they need the help of economists, and other scientists, in shaping new ways of living. The church that was founded by the one who had no place to lay his head had best not fail to help the new pioneers understand the spirit that is moving them into a new approach to life.

The End of the Beginning

We began this excursion into the recent rise of a new outlook on what is truly beautiful, good, valuable, and desirable with a survey of what we once liked to see in the movies and what has survived today. We passed to illustrations of life-styles that are significantly different from what, in Thoreau's words, are generally acclaimed as successful. Along the way we have surveyed the kind of society we have come to enjoy—or not enjoy—and perhaps have given some reasons why an alternative life-style is an understandable goal for thousands today. Perhaps you, the reader, are considering making a break, chucking the "normal" style of life and beginning your search for personal fulfillment. If you are, it may help you in your resolve to know that others besides the people mentioned in this book have "gotten free" and let go the dreams (or illusions) of the millions and found the happiness that eludes so many. After considerable experimentation in alternative life-styles myself, and a good deal of travel around the country, I can honestly say that elements (at least) of the simpler life-style are practiced by a very large part of the American population. The poor are often astute in this regard, for they have to be, and the lower middle class is frequently very good at alternatives since such knowledge is the only thing that keeps them in the middle class. People build their own houses or repair their own dwellings themselves. They refinish furniture, shop carefully for sales (even at discount stores), buy goods at the end of a season, can their own fruits and vegetables, hunt game, and sew their own clothing.

One couple I know has taken over an old house and is refurbishing it slowly, doing all the work themselves as they can afford the materials. The job is so extensive that they have projected a seven-year plan to complete it. Meanwhile, they are not unhappy, but happy and content because they have something worthwhile to do, are doing it themselves and for themselves. Their project is a family affair—and their family is the better for it.

Without being too immodest, I can say, too, that my family has experimented with alternative life-styles now for some years. We have moved, stepped down from high-paying jobs, majored in garage sales, and settled in a smaller town. We have found that we have prospered as we moved further away from the security of large institutions, since what you make matters less than what you spend. Our life has been more satisfying and far from dull as we have ventured out into the new.

If you aren't sure just what a plainer, simpler life involves, let me suggest that you read some of these books during your summer vacation or over the long winter nights. I offer them only to help you, as I hope this book has helped you to see that beauty is not in the shape of the person or in the style of the clothes and that a good life does not consist alone in what one owns.

Look at a *Holy Bible* and note Amos and Hosea. Look at Jesus' teachings in Matthew, Mark, and Luke.

In a different vein, read Harry Browne's *How I Found Freedom in an Unfree World* (Macmillan Company, 1973).

Shifting to the beautiful, read Eliot Wigginton's *The Foxfire Book* and *Foxfire 2* (Anchor Books, 1972 and 1973).

These books will tell you how the simple people of the southern mountains care for themselves and enjoy life.

Along the same line, of arts and crafts, yet with the thrust of the modern Woodstock generation, read *Woodstock Craftsman's Manual* by Jean Young (Praeger Publishers, 1972) and *Woodstock Craftsman's Manual 2* (1973), also by Jean Young.

Finally, look over *The Garage Sale Manual* by Jean and Jim Young (Praeger, 1973) which is published on recycled paper and may give you some ideas to recycle and reclaim your life.

Don't go off half-cocked; read up on things. Take some trips around areas of the country that interest you. There is a lot of empty land in Maine, the Pacific Northwest, and the Southwest. Take your time and come to your senses before you lose your mind.

NOTES

INTRODUCTION
1. Dorothy Kalins, *Cutting Loose* (New York: Saturday Review Press, 1973).
2. Harry Browne, *How I Found Freedom in an Unfree World* (New York: Macmillan, 1973).
3. Ibid.

CHAPTER 1 THE PRIDE OF POSSESSION
1. Jacques Ellul, *The Meaning of the City* (Grand Rapids, Mich.: William B. Eerdmans, 1970).
2. Daniel Yankelovich, "The New Naturalism," *Saturday Review* (Apr. 1, 1972), pp. 32ff.
3. Ibid.

CHAPTER 2 THE REVOLT AGAINST CONFORMITY
1. John C. Cooper, "The Black Man's Burden," *Metanoia*, Vol. 4, No. 1 (Mar. 1972).
2. John C. Cooper, *The Turn Right* (Philadelphia: Westminster Press, 1970).
3. Rollo May, *Power and Innocence* (New York: W. W. Norton, 1972).
4. Carlos Castaneda, *The Teachings of Don Juan—A Yaqui Way of Knowledge* (New York: Ballantine Books, 1971); *A Separate Reality, Further Conversations with Don Juan* (New York: Pocket Books, 1972); *Journey to Ixtlan—The Lessons of Don Juan* (New York: Simon & Schuster, 1972).
5. John C. Cooper, *Religion in the Age of Aquarius* (Philadelphia: Westminster Press, 1971).

CHAPTER 3 THE REACTION AGAINST BOTH CONFORMITY AND REVOLUTION
1. John C. Cooper, *The New Mentality* (Philadelphia: Westminster Press, 1969).
2. John C. Cooper, *The Turn Right* (Philadelphia: Westminster Press, 1970); *A New Kind of Man* (Philadelphia: Westminster Press, 1972); *The Recovery of America* (Philadelphia: Westminster Press, 1973).
3. Cooper, *A New Kind of Man.*
4. *Advertising Age* (Feb. 5, 1973).
5. See "Don Juan and the Sorcerer's Apprentice," *Time* (Mar. 5, 1973), p. 38.
6. Carlos Castaneda, *Journey to Ixtlan—The Lessons of Don Juan* (New York: Simon & Schuster, 1972).
7. Kathleen Kinkade, "Twin Oaks, A Walden-Two Experiment," *Psychology Today*, Vol. 6, No. 8 (Jan. 1973).
8. Ibid.
9. Helen and Scott Nearing, *Living the Good Life* (New York: Schocken Books, 1954).
10. David and Debbie Wilson, *Wall Street Journal,* July 13, 1971.

CHAPTER 4 TWO CULTURES IN COLLISION
1. John A. Hostetler, *Amish Society* (Baltimore: Johns Hopkins Press, 1968), pp. 28ff.
2. Ibid.
3. William I. Schreiber, *Our Amish Neighbors* (Chicago: University of Chicago Press, 1962). pp. 77ff.
4. Ibid.
5. John C. Cooper, *The Recovery of America* (Philadelphia: Westminster Press, 1973).
6. Michael Novak, *The Rise of Unmeltable Ethnics* (New York: Macmillan, 1972).
7. Dean M. Kelley, *Why Conservative Churches Are Growing* (New York: Harper & Row, 1972).
8. Ibid., p. 12.
9. Ibid., p. 13.
10. Ibid., p. 20.
11. Ibid., p. 37.
12. Ibid., p. 57.
13. Ibid., p. 77.
14. Ibid., p. 164.
15. Ibid., p. 176.

CHAPTER 5 ART AND THE NEW PLAINNESS
1. See the following articles: Sam Keen, "Sorcerer's Apprentice," *Psychology Today*, Vol. 6, No. 7 (Dec. 1972); *Time*, Vol. 101, No. 10 (Mar. 5, 1973), cover story.

2. Dietrich Bonhoeffer, *Ethics*, ed. Eberhard Bethge (New York: Macmillan, 1965).
3. T. C. McLuhan, ed., *Touch the Earth* (New York: Outerbridge, 1971).
4. Ibid., p. 23. The speech is by Walking Buffalo, a Stoney Indian of Canada.
5. Paul Tillich, *Systematic Theology,* 3 vols. in one (Chicago: University of Chicago Press, 1957). See Utopianism: Vol. II, pp. 30, 42, 74, 86; Vol. III, pp. 345-46, 353-55, 358, 360, 387.
6. Nena and George O'Neill, *Open Marriage, a New Life Style for Couples* (New York: M. Evans & Co., 1972).
7. Ibid., pp. 252, 256-57.
8. Ibid., pp. 260ff.
9. Ibid.

CHAPTER 6 FEED YOUR HEAD—A NATURAL PHILOSOPHY

1. T. C. McLuhan, ed., *Touch the Earth* (New York: Outerbridge, 1971).
2. Gordon P. Harding, "So We Came to Vermont," *The Grinnell Magazine,* Grinnell College, Iowa (Mar.-Apr. 1973), pp. 8-9.
3. *The Philadelphia Inquirer* (Dec. 10, 1971).
4. Ibid.
5. *The Toledo Blade,* Sunday Magazine, (Aug. 19, 1973), pp. 16ff.
6. George Steiner, from an interview in *Psychology Today*, Vol. 6, No. 9 (Feb. 1973), pp. 56-69.
7. Rollo May, *Power and Innocence* (New York: W. W. Norton, 1972).
8. Daniel J. Boorstin, *The Americans: The Democratic Experience* (New York: Random House, 1973), pp. 3-88.
9. *Walden, The Writings of Henry David Thoreau* (New York: Houghton Mifflin Co., 1906.)
10. Jean and Jim Young, *The Garage Sale Manual* (New York: Praeger, 1973).